DOUGLAS WEISS, PH.D.

PRODIGAL PARENT
process

Prodigal Parent Process
Copyright © 2021 by Douglas Weiss, Ph.D.

Requests for information:
Discovery Press
heart2heart@xc.org
719-278-3708

Interior and Cover designed by Janelle Evangelides

Printed in the United States of America
ISBN #978-1-881292-44-9

Contents

INTRODUCTION

There are moms and dads in every church who suffer deeply because of a prodigal child in their family. Most Sundays, as the music fills the sanctuary and the sermon is delivered, their minds and souls wander off into the private pain of envisioning their prodigal traveling an undesirable road. The vacant seat next to them stirs the void in their heart.

They scroll through the memories of when their child came to church, sang songs, and worshipped God. They remember the family Bible studies and the bedside prayers. They do not understand how this once godly child can now yell at them, call them names, and behave so defiantly. Even worse, they do not understand the resistance to sharing a meal or having a simple conversation.

These wounded parents are in every church. Some are silent. Some ask for prayer. Most are enduring the grief of losing their daughter or son.

This book is created for Christian parents of prodigal children to help them understand what went wrong, acknowledge the truth, embrace hope and begin to heal. Through this teaching, you will learn the actual and biblical reality of how a person (or, more aptly, a soul) chooses to become a prodigal and the steps you can take to heal from the trauma of the broken relationship. Additionally, you will discover ways to improve your relationship once your prodigal chooses to come home.

As you read, I hope you heal and become stronger for your spouse, family, and even your child. God is aware of the decisions and actions of your prodigal and the pain that it causes you. He desires to have His child, who is on loan to you, return home to Him as well.

Douglas Weiss, Ph.D.

CHAPTER
One

THE FIRST PRODIGAL PARENT

Every lousy story begins with a good one. In the beginning, God created. And with that, we are drawn into the greatest story ever told. It has a miraculous beginning, awful middle, and fantastic ending. This magnificent creation account is simultaneously the story of God and the story of us. The buildup is immense. He speaks, and the waters separate; stars fill the sky; plants and creatures flourish.

Then in the second chapter of Genesis, God slows down. He thoughtfully and carefully forms His eternal son born in time, Adam. He raises him to become a man of service, trains him to work the land, and directs him to name the animals. Then

God creates Eve and gives her to Adam, and in doing so, God creates marriage—the trinity on earth as it is in heaven.

The stage is set! An amazing God has prepared all of creation for His children. A perfect Father loves and spends quality time with Adam and Eve. He teaches them, gives them responsibility for the land and animals, and established only one command: live at peace in His garden.

As this epic story unfolds, we see a sinless man and woman living in the perfect love and care of an all-powerful God, and then, WHAMO! Like a knockout punch from Rocky Balboa, the reader is taken into the painful abyss of a story gone rogue. This perfect, beautiful, godly, strong, brilliant couple with endless resources hits the dust through sin, and their epic beginning gives way to a tragic journey.

The Father who spent who knows how long convincing the Son and the Holy Spirit to create a free will race is now the first prodigal parent in history. And despite His pain, God sticks to His word; because of their disobedience, Adam and Eve would experience many types of suffering and even death. He has them escorted out of the Garden of Eden, and He, like many of you reading this, is now a parent to prodigals. How did this happen?

> ¹Now the serpent was more crafty than any of the wild animals the LORD God had made. He said to the woman, "Did God really say, 'You must not eat from any tree in the garden'?" ²The woman said to the serpent, "We may eat fruit from the trees in the garden, ³but God did say, 'You must not eat fruit from the tree that is in the middle of the garden, and you must not touch it, or you will die.'" ⁴"You will not certainly die," the serpent said to the woman. ⁵"For God knows that when you eat from it your eyes will be opened, and you will be like God, knowing good and evil."

> Genesis 3:1-5

The Father, Son, and Holy Spirit, perfect in every way, have created us to live in a beautiful relationship with them. And—for their glory and our good—they created a moral universe where choices have consequences. And they gave us the ability to choose. So it was with Adam and Eve. These first prodigals made their choice and received the consequences. Adam went from a supernatural, abundant lifestyle where everything was provided for him to a life of daily laboring and striving for his sustenance. And Eve went from the perfect helpmate to being ruled over by her husband and having to endure greater pain in childbirth.

The Father did everything He could do to have His children live with him for eternity. He felt pain when He was rejected. His heart was broken. He endured being misunderstood, slandered, and taken advantage of—much like the parents of prodigal children. I draw your attention to this parallel; it helps us to understand that God, your Father, not only understands your pain but feels it with you.

"

GOD, YOUR FATHER, NOT ONLY UNDERSTANDS
YOUR PAIN BUT FEELS IT WITH YOU.

Just as the Father *created* the world and the garden for His children, parents anticipate and create a world for their children to live in. Inevitably, moms and dads share the excitement of a new soul entering this world; they get rooms ready, wonder how to make more money, and manage more responsibilities. You both kicked in money toward all the preparations, such as the baby furniture, clothes, and bottles. And when the baby came, it was an all-out effort to feed, clothe and care for your child. Your house was full of baby bottles, clothes, and furniture. You were so proud. You may have had them dedicated at church. You showed them off to everyone who would listen.

In the same way, God *invests* in His children, parents, regardless of how much income they earn, invest a huge percentage of their money toward caring for and raising children. It begins with food, clothing, and housing, and it continues with developing their unique gifts through classes, practices, sports, music, and school events. You invested in their hobbies, cars, and college. And you were glad you did.

And like God, who gives His *time* to His children, parents sacrifice hours, weeks, months, and years of their lives to be with their children. It is not just holidays, birthdays, and other special occasions; it is walks, bike rides, watching movies, playing board games, fixing things, and cooking. And all of this was to express your love in so many ways. Some of you raised your children to follow Christ. You brought them to a church where they were baptized, sang in the choir, or even taught Sunday School to younger children. You invested spiritual energy to move them closer to loving and serve Jesus Christ.

While there are many similarities between the first parent of a prodigal, God the Father, and Christian prodigal parents, there is also a significant difference. I have been counseling for three decades now, and I have been in the Church since I was nineteen. I have met and counseled many prodigal sons and daughters; many had run far from God and their families. I have cared for countless parents whose children have walked away from them and God. It is excruciatingly painful to experience the prodigal parent process. And parents who are enduring this process without a good biblical grounding can become very emotional, toxic, and even destructive to your marriage and the rest of the family.

Since we know the story, let's examine the idea of the prodigal parent process focusing on the first prodigal parent— God—since He was the first to endure His children's disobedience and separation. In identifying how He handled His children's decisions, we can gain insight into how parents of prodigals may want to handle their prodigal. Additionally, it may be helpful to honestly compare your perspective on and reaction to having a prodigal child with that of God's.

Let's begin with the several things the Father <u>did not do</u>.

First, God did not take any responsibility for His children's choices. He gave them free will; He gave them one law (so to speak) with a known consequence if they broke that law. When they broke that command, He did not take any responsibility for their actions. He did not blame Himself.

"

GOD DID NOT TAKE ANY RESPONSIBILITY FOR HIS CHILDREN'S CHOICES.

Second, God did not blame anyone else. He didn't blame the Holy Spirit for not being enough. He didn't even blame the snake for His children's behaviors. God does not blame anyone for His children's behavior except them.

Third, God did not question His parenting. He did not say, "Where did I go wrong?" "I didn't provide enough or do enough." "I wasn't there for them." "I know somehow I could have been a better parent." God did not look inward for causality that was independent of Him.

Fourth, He did not beg or plead for them to change their minds. He didn't intervene while they were contemplating their choice. He didn't create rain, thunder, or a bright light—nothing! He granted them free will and allowed them to use it even if it wasn't in their best interest.

Fifth, He administered the consequences immediately. Adam and Eve did not escape the costs of their choices. Still to this day, man toils in his work, and women have pain in childbirth. God did not chase after them in the garden. And perhaps because I am a counselor by profession, I can say that God had zero co-dependent behaviors with his prodigal children.

As a parent, He acknowledged their sin as *their* sin. He didn't sugarcoat it or have any form of denial. This is critical in the prodigal parent process.

The more you assume responsibility when it is not yours, the harder the prodigal parent process will be. The more you blame yourself or others, the more difficult this journey will be for you and possibly your marriage and family. Many well-intentioned Christian parents fail to follow the biblical model of acknowledging free will and the consequences therein. Instead, they seek to protect their children by blaming themselves, others, or a situation as to why their son or daughter became a prodigal.

> **THE MORE YOU ASSUME RESPONSIBILITY WHEN IT IS NOT YOURS, THE HARDER THE PARENT PRODIGAL PROCESS WILL BE.**

As a parent, you may not want to give your child full responsibility for their choice to be a prodigal. But it is important to understand that God always provides a way out for us so we can choose not to sin (see 1 Corinthians 10:13). When we sin, it's a choice—even amid or as a result of pain, abuse, and trauma. When trials come, one soul may choose secrecy and sin and move away from God, and another soul may move into openness and draw close to God. We always have a choice. Your children have a choice and the freedom to make it.

> **"**
>
> MANY WELL-INTENTIONED CHRISTIAN PARENTS FAIL TO FOLLOW THE BIBLICAL MODEL OF ACKNOWLEDGING FREE WILL AND THE CONSEQUENCES THEREIN.

In reflecting on God's relationship with Adam and Eve and His actions as a parent of a prodigal, we can embrace the freedom that comes from knowing how a perfect Father cares for His children, knowing that He cares for us and is helping us be more like Him. And this includes our parenting decisions.

You are not alone; millions of parents have prodigal children; so does God. You have a Heavenly Father who understands and feels the pain of a child's choice to be a prodigal. Your child is not only a prodigal toward you but also toward the Father.

You are not to blame. God does not blame you. I do not blame you. You can learn not to blame yourself. In the coming chapters, we will look at this truth from various angles so you can begin to understand the prodigal process, the biblical truth it represents, and the hope of living with a heavenly Father who understands. I believe you can gain clarity as to how your child became a prodigal and gain some tools to better go through many of the experiences parents of prodigals need to navigate.

My hope is by the end of this book, you can feel whole as you walk through this part of your story with Christ.

CHAPTER
Two
THE PRODIGAL AND GOD

As a prodigal parent, I believe it is very important for you to understand the prodigal process. The prodigal process is a clear and identifiable process that any soul can choose at any time.

For a moment, I want you to suspend all your preconceived notions as to why your child became a prodigal or who might have caused or contributed to their decision. I want to demystify the prodigal process. How? By sharing a similar process that is more commonly acknowledged.

Nearly every week, it seems, I counsel godly women whose husbands cheat on them or look at pornography. This is often their only experience of being betrayed by their husband and not knowing what to do. They often blame themselves, the "other woman," society, or even the devil. It is very common for women to feel relieved after I explain the six types of sex addicts and how this likely started well before she met him. Then I explain the word of God in James 1:15: "Then, after desire has conceived, it gives birth to sin; and sin, when it is full-grown, gives birth to death." Notice the progression—the process—from lust to sin to death (lust is like a seed with guaranteed fruit regardless of who you marry). When these women believe the word of God, it starts to demystify their situations and enables them to recognize their husband's responsibility for their poor choices.

A second reason I want to share the prodigal process with you is to help you pray through this situation. God is longing for your child to come back to Him and to you. That is His heart and perfect will.

The final reason I want to share the prodigal process with you is to have a clear, biblically-based understanding of a prodigal. If your beliefs are not biblical, your thoughts and actions can be less helpful in this bizarre season you find yourself in.

GOD IS LONGING FOR YOUR CHILD TO COME BACK TO HIM
AND TO YOU. THAT IS HIS HEART AND PERFECT WILL.

I find that parents who clearly understand the path all prodigals take are less likely to assume any false responsibility. The parent who understands the biblical process of the prodigal is often free from blaming themselves, their spouses, or others for the prodigal's choices.

This biblical freedom can help you to walk through your prodigal parent process more easily. When we read 2 Corinthians 3:17, we learn God is the source of freedom: "...and where the Spirit of the Lord is there is freedom." I find when we believe the truth of God's Word, regardless of our feelings, we are free.

I often have clients who, because of circumstances or because of their own feelings of worthlessness, make poor choices. To help them identify the truth about who they are, I encourage them to watch the DVD called *Worthy,* which focuses on bringing freedom to anyone who has struggled with doubting their amazing worth. When they believe God's

Word that we are worth the blood of Christ because He says we are, they can change the way they think and feel.

In this very same way, when a parent believes God's Word on how a prodigal becomes a prodigal, their thoughts and behavior change. This freedom is my hope for you as I explain the prodigal process.

THE PRODIGAL PROCESS

Often as I read God's Word, He shows me processes. To understand what I see, I will go over it again and again, often reading several translations and writing flow charts, and it's like a big WOW... that's a process in the Word of God! Discovering the prodigal process was one of these moments.

I want to take you through a passage in Romans that clearly outlines what thousands of my clients have lived out in their lives. Get your Bible out and go to Romans 1:19: "...since what may be known about God is plain to them, because God has made it plain to them." This scripture makes it radically clear that every prodigal knows God. Every prodigal knows God because God Himself, in some way or in many ways, has revealed Himself to everyone, including your prodigal.

In many cases, if you were Christians when raising your child, they were exposed to God, His heart, His thoughts, His will, and His love. You taught them about Jesus; others in the church taught them about the Holy Spirit; your child absolutely knows God (or at least of God). Even a soul like mine, where I never heard about God in my family, God made Himself known to me. I know that God does the work of revealing Himself. Regardless of how well you thought you, your spouse, or your church did with your prodigal, God revealed Himself to your son or daughter. My experience is He is really good at revealing Himself to His children.

GOD IS REALLY GOOD AT REVEALING HIMSELF TO HIS CHILDREN.

The first step in the prodigal's journey is that they know God. This is important because it is not that God, you, or your spouse failed your child in knowing God.

Continuing on in Romans 1, we identify the next step a prodigal must take to go down the path of becoming a prodigal. Verse 21 claims, "For although they knew God, they neither glorified him as God nor gave thanks to him, but their thinking became futile, and their foolish hearts were darkened." This scripture reaffirms that it is a commonplace for people to know God—because God makes it possible—and it walks step-by-step how people, by their own choosing, make themselves a prodigal. I want to walk through the first five steps of a prodigal.

Step One:

"...they did not glorify God as God." This means they did not give Him pre-eminence in the first place. They did not worship Him from their heart. This is not something you, as a parent, could ever know about the heart of your child. This is what we do when we are alone with God. This is us fulfilling the first commandment to have no other gods before us (see Exodus 20:3).

Many of the prodigals I have treated shared how they would say the right things around their parents and in church, even though they did not believe what they were saying. The prodigal, in their heart, says, "No, you are not God to me. You might be God, but not to me."

As we walk through this prodigal process, I want you to see the prodigal process is entirely about that person's relationship with God and nothing else.

<u>Step Two:</u>

The scripture continues, "nor gave thanks to Him" (v. 21). This is a very common denominator of prodigals—they are generally ungrateful. They first push God away in their heart, and a symptom of that is they are not grateful for their health, blessings, finances, family, or much of anything. Think about your own experience long before you knew of their double life. Was there a growing attitude of thanklessness?

Now before I go onto the next step, I want to highlight something to you. The prodigal process is fully *independent* of your parenting. The prodigal process is entirely a heart process, not a parenting process.

"

THE PRODIGAL PROCESS IS ENTIRELY A HEART PROCESS,
NOT A PARENTING PROCESS.

<u>*Step Three:*</u>

The third step of choosing to be a prodigal is "their thinking became futile" (v. 21). Futile means that their thinking is not capable of producing a result. So many parents have said about their prodigal: "They just do not make any sense." "They are going nowhere, and they cannot even see it."

The bizarre way prodigals process information (or, better, misprocess information) is a direct result of rejecting God. So too is what they believe about themselves and the world. This deficiency in their thinking-process issue is not a result of your parenting. When we step away from God being our foundation, doubting that He exists or that He is the one we are ultimately accountable to, our hearts and actions walk away from this reality and truth of who God is, even though we know because He has made Himself known.

When your premise (foundation) is incorrect, your conclusion will also be incorrect. You will think that your prodigal's thoughts are off, interesting, bizarre, even illogical or crazy, but they will believe that their way of thinking is correct and that you are old-fashioned, a bigot, religious and close-minded. They believe this thinking in their heart, so you cannot win a fight with them because they believe what they think. As the scripture says, "They just do not make any sense."

Step Four:

The fourth step of a soul choosing to reject God and choosing to be a prodigal is significant. In this step, the scripture says, "and their foolish hearts were darkened" (v. 21). The heart is the most powerful part of our being. Our heart is where we believe. The heart is where we believe in Christ and are saved. Proverbs 4:23 tells us to "Above all else, guard your heart, for everything you do flows from it." I believe the heart is the very rudder of our soul.

The heart leads the mind, will, and emotions. I have seen souls make decisions in their hearts and shipwreck themselves, so when the scripture says that the heart becomes darkened, this is serious. This darkened heart can show up in several ways to you as a parent. Children may gravitate to friendships with other people who also have darkened hearts (our friends deeply reflect our beliefs and values).

Their darkened heart can also attract darkened romantic/sexual relationships. The darkened heart might also choose to get involved in drugs, cultish behaviors, illegal activities, or a myriad of activities that Bible-believing Christians are instructed to flee from. As a parent, going through this prodigal process is challenging. This process has a face and a name, and it belongs to the child you love. However, regardless of who they are and how much they are loved, this is the prodigal process the scripture lays out for us to understand. And again, the prodigal is making a choice.

Step Five:

The fifth step in the process is found in Romans 1:22-23: "Although they claimed to be wise, they became fools and exchanged the glory of the immortal God for images made to look like a mortal human being and birds and animals and reptiles." The heart needs to believe something. When a prodigal rejects the person of God, their heart seeks out other ideas to root their beliefs. This can move them to pick up a cause—often political or religious—and they can become a zealot for that particular cause or group. They could also start investigating other religions, formally or informally. They could become advocates for humanism or "the good life." Anything or any idea could become preeminent for their hearts. You could see a significant shift in values around sex, money, politics, religion, worldviews, and creation. There is no telling where the heart will go to find value in something or someone. As a parent, you can feel lost and powerless. They fully believe these new ideas, having discarded the old ones. You, again, can try to argue with them, but these are heart beliefs. So, logic or truth will contribute little toward changing them. They will have to have a heart change for them to change their beliefs.

"

WHEN A PRODIGAL REJECTS THE PERSON OF GOD, THEIR HEART SEEKS OUT OTHER IDEAS TO ROOT THEIR BELIEFS.

The remainder of Romans Chapter 1 explains how a prodigal can get into more sexual immorality and idolatry. For some prodigals, the journey is slow, and they move through this over the years; however, for others prodigals, the journey is rapid. Relating to the speed at which it rejects God and moves into other beliefs or behaviors, every soul is different.

THEY WILL HAVE TO HAVE A HEART CHANGE FOR THEM TO CHANGE THEIR BELIEFS.

Now, I want you to pause and think about what you read about the prodigal process. Consider what the scripture indicates about the prodigal process and who is involved? What do you see? Yes, that's right; parents were nowhere mentioned in the prodigal process! There is not one place where it places blame on the dad who didn't spend time with his son or daughter or didn't play ball or go to a game. There isn't one reference to the mother not being loving or kind. There is no correlation between parenting and why the child rejected God and became a prodigal. From a biblical perspective, parents are not a variable. Now you can make it up and emotionally buy into the idea that you or your spouse are to blame, but you won't find a scripture to support that thought.

Now, like the prodigal, if a parent's premise or foundation is wrong, so is their conclusion, even if they emotionally believe it's true. I find so many parents start with the idea that they somehow created this prodigal situation. A prodigal is a prodigal because they choose to be a prodigal.

Let's review the prodigal process:

1. Each prodigal knows God.
2. Each prodigal rejects God as God.
3. The prodigal changes the way he/she thinks, feels, and believes.
4. The prodigal's hearts get darker.
5. The prodigal's behavior gets darker.

These are steps the heart of the prodigal takes to become a prodigal. You, as a parent, are not a variable in the prodigal process. Here are a few conclusions that are biblical in the prodigal process.

First, the biblical process of being a prodigal is a known process. You can see it through the story of Israel in the Old Testament repeatedly. Again and again, they rejected God, ignored His commands, and pursue idols and sexual immorality.

Second, the prodigal process is a heart choice. This is good news: if a heart can choose to reject God, it can also, at another point, choose to accept God and follow Him whole-heartedly. A prodigal, regardless of how long they have been away or how dark their life has become, is one belief away from returning. As parents, focus your prayers on your child's heart. It's the heart of the prodigal that must put God first. Once the heart changes, the mind, behavior and friendships will all start to change.

"

IF A HEART CAN CHOOSE TO REJECT GOD, IT CAN ALSO, AT ANOTHER POINT, CHOOSE TO ACCEPT GOD AND FOLLOW HIM WHOLE-HEARTEDLY.

Lastly, the prodigal process is curable. We all have heard the stories of how a prodigal has come back to Christ. Many of the most passionate believers in Christ were prodigals. The prodigal can always come back to God. I have seen thousands of souls reverse the prodigal process. They first put God back in His rightful place as Lord. They then become thankful for salvation and move towards a servant's heart. Their minds become clearer as their hearts move toward the light God is showing them, and they can become pure in heart again. Their beliefs, relationships, sexual behaviors all begin to clear up. They become "oaks of righteousness" (Isaiah 61:3) and mature at an incredible rate. I have experienced this reversal in myself and have witnessed thousands of prodigals come home.

Your experience with your prodigal will be unique to you; however, as you go through each of the following chapters, I am hoping you can see that the prodigal process is not unique—it is very clear, and it is independent of you and your spouse. You did not cause this prodigal situation. As you continue to read, you will be given more insights and tools to walk through this process with more skill, with no self-blame, and a growing ability to love the soul has walked away from the Father, their truest parent.

CHAPTER
Three

THE PRODIGAL SON

By far, the most famous story of a prodigal was taught by our Master and Savior, Jesus. The "prodigal son" story, as it has been taught and preached all around the world, has much to teach us.

In this chapter, I want to focus on the prodigal son. In the future chapters, I will discuss the father and the older brother in the story. As we examine the scripture, keep in mind that I already shared how the prodigal is in the process of rebellion against God and how this plays out in their ungratefulness, improper thinking, and their behaviors.

Let's read through Luke 15, a small section at a time. In doing so, you will see the prodigal process we already looked at as outlined in Romans 1. We will begin with verses 11-12: "Jesus continued: 'There was a man who had two sons. The younger one said to his father, "Father, give me my share of the estate." So, he divided his property between them.'" When you look at this scripture, it's clear the younger son has, in his heart, already gone down the road of the prodigal. He didn't consult God about his lust for his father's estate. He didn't say God was leading him in any manner. God was not at all part of this son's worldview at this point. So, we see this prodigal already didn't have God at the center of his thoughts. Even the well-known command to "honor your father and mother" (Exodus 20:15) wasn't a part of this prodigal's decision.

You see, one of the effects of being a prodigal is other people lose their value—people become objects (more on this later). This prodigal did not have God in the right place in his heart.

Next, you clearly see the thanklessness and entitlement. This son had no share in an estate as long as his father lived. His entitlement created crazy thinking and a darkened heart. Children have no rights to an estate at all. This is how delusional it is being a prodigal.

As a parent, your prodigal might have asked or demanded of you to pay for something—a house, car, vacation, or electronics. You might have felt used if they began to only interact with you when they wanted something. You might have been betrayed financially and emotionally as well.

Because they reject the lordship of God, the prodigal is not in their right state of mind. This state of being is not because of your parenting. This father in the story was the father to both boys, and the other was not delusional or entitled in this way at all. You see, it's not parenting. Being a prodigal is a choice.

"

BEING A PRODIGAL IS A CHOICE.

Let's continue in verse 13: "Not long after that, the younger son got together all he had, set off for a distant country and there squandered his wealth in wild living." This young man was quick to get together "all that he had." This boy wasn't planning a vacation; he was planning to leave for good. This, again, reflects a heart issue.

I have worked with prodigals for over thirty years, and when they have it in their heart to sin and sin big, they don't want any accountability. They don't want to answer to anyone on where they've been, who they were with, or what they were doing. They want to live in a world of their making where they are gods and answer to no one. They don't want to be around godly or principled parents, siblings, neighbors, church members, or even teachers who would remind them that they are not living right. This is important, as so many parents blame themselves for being the reason why the prodigal wants to leave home; they take the rejection personally. It's not personal; it's business! They want to sin, and they don't want anyone to try to stop them. Their heart is hell-bent on this commitment to "get out of Dodge" and do as they please. They are intentionally removing any godly or even reasonable authority from their lives. This includes siblings. The prodigal didn't just leave the dad; he left a godly brother as well. People and relationships have no value as a prodigal's thoughts become futile, and their hearts become darkened.

Now, understand this boy wasn't given a few hundred dollars: he was given a large inheritance. His father owned and was running a large farm with many servants. What this means for traditional Jewish families in that day and age is the father had to sell a portion of the land he owned in order to give this prodigal son his share of the assumed future inheritance. This took time, but once this transaction between the father and the new owner was complete, this prodigal son was probably given the equivalent of several hundred thousand dollars in today's money. Rather than being grateful, he continued in with his hard-heartedness, and he went off to another country, perhaps with a horse and some donkeys. We can also surmise that he traveled for weeks or months to get to a "far-off country."

> **"**
>
> PEOPLE AND RELATIONSHIPS HAVE NO VALUE AS A PRODIGAL'S THOUGHTS BECOME FUTILE, AND THEIR HEARTS BECOME DARKENED.

In verse 13, we learn he spent all of his money on wild living. In verse 30, the older brother clarifies this further, "But when this son of yours who has squandered your property with prostitutes..." Here we see a young man out of control: drinking, partying, and paying for sex. He could easily be seen as someone with an alcohol or sexual addiction. You see, he had enough money to buy a small vineyard or buy a business, get married, generating income, and still drink responsibly; however, he didn't create wealth. He didn't know how, and only an addict-type person could party that hard into total irresponsible poverty and not stop before he hit bottom, or better said, bottom hit him.

I once heard a preacher say money makes you more of who you are. I think that is true. If you are responsible or kind, you are likely to become more responsible and kind. If you are self-absorbed and irresponsible, more money can and probably will make you more self-absorbed and irresponsible. Like time, money is a measure of our values. Watch how your prodigal spends time and money—this will give insight into their heart's condition.

Your prodigal may or may not be an addict (we will discuss that later); however, if you feel your prodigal is out of control, can't see the impact of their decisions, is hanging around the wrong people and doing things they were raised to not do, then you can relate to this process that they are examining.

Remember, the prodigal process is independent of you. The prodigal process is about rejecting God, and that means getting away from anything that has the aroma of God, including their parents and family.

> THE PRODIGAL PROCESS IS ABOUT REJECTING GOD, AND THAT MEANS GETTING AWAY FROM ANYTHING THAT HAS THE AROMA OF GOD, INCLUDING THEIR PARENTS AND FAMILY.

It is very common for prodigals to have a secret in their teen years that their parents are clueless about. The secret might be smoking, drugs, pornography, sexual abuse, rape, an eating disorder, alcohol abuse, or a bizarre relationship. The secret keeps growing, and like James 1:15 tells us: first lust, then sin, and then death. Often the prodigal stage is when things move from the inner life (lust) to the outer life (behavior). As a parent, you may wonder, "How did this happen?" For the prodigal's friends or siblings, it makes total sense. A little sin became a bigger sin, just like a seed becoming a plant.

This parable in Luke 15 shares not only how someone chooses to become a prodigal but also how they can come back. As Jesus continues to tell the story,

He tells the rest of the story —one of hope. This coming home is also a known process that millions of prodigals have taken to come back to the Father.

Jesus continues in verse 14, "After he had spent everything..." This is classic. A prodigal will go as far as they can on self-will, spending, making poor choices, and eventually, there's a bottom and an end of their resources. Not only are they at an end financially and emotionally, but they have likely severed all the relationships they could manipulate in the past. In Alcoholics Anonymous, they call this event hitting bottom. This is where the prodigal is beginning to discover and think about the possibility that what they are doing isn't working for them anymore.

Then Jesus adds an interesting event, "...there was a severe famine in that whole country, and he began to be in need" (v. 14). This statement is so fascinating to me. You have to ask yourself, who creates famine? Repeatedly, God shares that He created a famine or that He will. Only God, our great God, can create a famine (see *Ezekiel 14:12-23; Amos 8:11; Acts 11:28; Revelation 6:8).*

God will create national and international events to help a prodigal. Your God is working to intervene with your child, inviting them to come back to Him. In this case, the famine dried up the resources of this prodigal; otherwise, he might have stayed longer in his sinful state. As a point of prayer, you can agree with God to create the circumstances that can bring about the heart change; however, these circumstances are not always pleasant for the prodigal.

"

GOD WILL CREATE NATIONAL AND INTERNATIONAL EVENTS TO HELP A PRODIGAL

I also want to highlight the last statement of Jesus in verse 14, "...he began to be in need." So, the prodigal has to run out of reserves or hit bottom, and they must be in need. This prodigal went from living in abundance with his father to having wasted everything he had and being in need. Discovering they have a need they cannot satisfy on their own is often the very moment when the prodigal begins to look for alternatives. This is a very important process as their heart is no longer agreeing with his life choices.

Continuing with the story, this prince of a boy, now a pauper, did what he could in his own strength to solve his problem while in a foreign country: he got a job feeding pigs. Luke 12:15–16 tells us, "So he went and hired himself out to a citizen of that country, who sent him to his fields to feed pigs. He longed to fill his stomach with the pods that the pigs were eating, but no one gave him anything."

This foreign boy prodigal was experiencing a few things. First, he was experiencing hunger with no real hope of change. This hopelessness of heart was probably a motivator. Second, he was experiencing what it was like to be treated as an object, have no value as a soul, just a thing, much like he treated his father and family. The scripture states that he was hungry, "but no one gave him anything." In other words, these people probably had some food but would not give this foreigner any help. He wasn't being treated as a person but as someone disdained.

Now, before we go into the son's coming back, I want to review the six points of a prodigal coming to his senses. Let's go through the steps:

1. He ran out of resources.
2. There was a severe famine (things got worse).

3. He became in need.

4. He experienced hunger and hopelessness.

5. He was treated the way he treated others.

6. He came to his senses.

What is glaringly missing from this process?

The parents! The parents were in no way a part of this darkened heart moving back toward the Father. His father didn't send a servant, write a note of encouragement or send money. So many parents want to be a part of the prodigal's process; however, I find zero biblical grounds for a parent being part of the process that involves God and His prodigal. Also, in thirty-plus years of prodigals telling me their stories of coming home to God the Father, I can't think of one story where the parents were involved until after the prodigal first came back to God. I'm not saying it can't happen; I'm just saying, biblically, I find no support for a parent bringing a child back. Before you get mad or send me an email, search your scriptures and see if you come to the same conclusion.

THE PARENTS WERE IN NO WAY A PART OF THIS DARKENED HEART MOVING BACK TOWARD THE FATHER.

Now, I want to return to our prodigal son's story. Jesus continues, "When he came to his senses..." (v. 17). A prodigal coming to his senses is often an internal response to a lot of painful external circumstances. I know I went through a very similar process to come to God. I had to realize that what I was doing wasn't working anymore.

> A PRODIGAL COMING TO HIS SENSES IS OFTEN AN INTERNAL RESPONSE TO A LOT OF PAINFUL EXTERNAL CIRCUMSTANCES.

Then in the same verse, the prodigal said, "How many of my father's hired servants have food to spare, and here I am starving to death!" Remember, this son is reflecting while being hungry, mistreated, broke, and out of options. As he reflects, he remembers even servants in his father's house are treated like people and live in more abundance than the self-willed life he was living with foreigners who didn't care for him at all.

For me, the next verse (18) clues me in that he might have an addict's mind or at least an opportunist edge to him because he came up with his "next plan." The prodigal son says, "I will set out and go back to my father and say to him: Father, I have sinned against heaven and against you." Let's stop here for a moment. Our prodigal not only came to his senses, but he realized he sinned against "heaven," and he repented. He was willing to accept God and that he was accountable to God. He also realized he sinned against his father. This is the order of repentance.

The prodigal also became aware he lives in a world where he is not God and that he needs to honor Him. He also realized people have value and that he had created pain for his father. And thus, He repented.

Rehearsing his speech, the prodigal says, "I am no longer worthy to be called your son; make me like one of your hired servants" (v. 19). And, "So he got up and went to his father" (v. 20). All this awareness came in a moment of self-reflection. There wasn't another person involved, not a preacher or parent, no one. He got to this point just between him and God. I'm grateful when God uses people to help facilitate heart change; I have been used by God in many of those moments. As a parent, it's ok to pray for your prodigal to have a heart reflection moment where they can see their circumstances clearly.

"

AS A PARENT, IT'S OK TO PRAY FOR YOUR PRODIGAL TO HAVE A HEART REFLECTION MOMENT WHERE THEY CAN SEE THEIR CIRCUMSTANCES CLEARLY.

And where was the prodigal son when he saw his circumstances? Where was he when he repented? He was in a field in a far-off foreign country. He wasted everything and likely had only a few pieces of clothing left as he headed home. He had to walk many miles. I imagine him humbling himself, asking for help; maybe he worked here and there along the journey to get food and water. He had to trust God to feed him. He had to trust other people to help. This was no fast track toward home. The prodigal returning home might also be a process of learning to trust God and others. I know after I got saved, I had no money, and God taught me to trust Him and others. This building of trust has been instrumental in my Christian walk.

As far as the prodigal goes, we know the rest of the story, and we will cover that in future chapters. After his long walk and reestablishing trust, the prodigal has returned home; his father received him and hosted a celebration. As parents, we will cover more of that part of the story in great detail later.

In this chapter, I wanted you again to be exposed to the idea that the prodigal journey is an independent choice of your child. Your prodigal will most likely go through a very similar painful process of self-discovery which will include acknowledging they are not God, they don't make the rules, and that they are here to serve God.

This prodigal process takes time. In the parable, this prodigal traveled. It took time for him to squander all the money. It took time for him to hit a place of need. It took quite a while for his walk home to his parent's house. As a parent, not one of us want our children to choose such a process for themselves. It's very hard to watch and not intervene as they make self-destructive poor choices, use drugs, get involved sexually, become confused, entitled, and ultimately in need. It's sad, but this is the prodigal process.

In Jesus' story, the prodigal follows the exact same pattern as we outlined in Romans 1. I trust that by seeing the process and examining the parable, you can eradicate any false blame toward yourself, your spouse, or others. You did not cause this, and you cannot cure this. This is an individual heart journey between a person and God. We, as parents, patiently watch the drama as a soul declares its independence from God and goes through the painful and sometimes prolonged process of finding God and coming home.

CHAPTER
Four
PROBLEMS FOR THE PRODIGAL

I know by now we have clearly established a couple of things. First, the prodigal process is an individual choice independent of your parenting. Secondly, the choice that every prodigal makes is to reject God as God. They don't allow Him to be their final authority, and now what they feel, think, believe, or misbelieve is entirely about the question, "Who is the absolute authority in my heart and life" (even if they might not use those words).

Most of the readers of this book will be Christians; most of you have raised your children to also follow Jesus. I know that what is happening is painful, embarrassing, scary, and makes you feel profoundly powerless. I want to help by inviting you to reflect on a question: When Israel repeatedly rejected God, what were the two most common consequences of this choice?

If you go page after page, prophetic warning after prophetic warning, you will find two themes that are evident in Israel's unfaithful relationship with God.

1. Israel would regularly get herself into sexual immorality when she left God. Israel would also get involved in various forms of idolatry with pagan gods.

2. The rejection of God has known consequences for a nation as well as for an individual prodigal.

Now, remember I am a psychologist. Prodigals like yours are in my office after their lives have encountered some form of crisis. As a prodigal, they can have a history of years or decades of poor choices. Depending on what that poor choice is, consistently over a long period of time, that ongoing choice can create addictions or other life-changing events. I'd like to share two stories.

Lori was fourteen when she started to push God way. It was slow at first. She still went to church, and she could speak "Christianese" around the family and church community. She started smoking cigarettes in high school and used the buzz to cope with feelings she wasn't talking about. In college, she drank a little, experimented with drugs, and engaged in some casual sex; however, smoking cigarettes was the one constant choice that she kept in her life. Then in her mid-twenties, she moved to Seattle, married a non-Christian, raised her children in a secular manner, and had strained relationships with her family in Dallas.

She spent over three decades as a prodigal. At age fifty-four, she was diagnosed with lung cancer because of her ongoing cigarette usage; she continued smoking even after her diagnosis. Over time she acknowledged she had created a nicotine addiction, so she went to a treatment center to get help. There she found God again and started her journey back to her faith and her family in Dallas.

Jon was sixty years old when he came to my office. He came back to Christ in my office, weeping profusely for his sins. You see, Jon started viewing pornography when he was about twelve years old. He kept this secret his whole life and always felt it kept him separated from God. Jon married a great Christian woman, and his family went to church, but he had a double life. He started having one-night stands early in his marriage, then a long-term affair, all while still using pornography several times a week. As his sexual addiction grew over the decades, he started paying prostitutes. Then he got caught!

After he was caught, he confessed the truth of his story, took a polygraph to validate he had stopped. Yes, he came back to Christ, but he now had to heal a sexual addiction he created as a result of habitual sin.

Why am I telling you these stories?

It is common for prodigals to create addictions in their lives as a result of pushing God away from their hearts. These addictions could be the obvious ones like alcohol, drugs, pornography, cigarettes, or gambling. There could also be subtler addictions that include work, video games, intimacy anorexia, food, or a multitude of others. Your prodigal can be in the early or later stages of an addiction. You may or may not be aware of their addiction; however, this addiction robs them of at least three significant areas of development: spiritual, emotional, and moral.

Their spiritual development can quickly stop at the age the addiction became active. Their emotional development likely stopped at the age of the addiction. You see, spiritually, the addict replaces God with the substance or the behavior. They go to the addiction for escape and comfort, not the Lord. Emotionally, instead of identifying feelings, feeling feelings, and talking about feelings to develop emotionally, the addict makes a different choice. When the addict has feelings, they get overwhelmed and pursue their substance or behavior of choice to numb whatever the feeling is so they don't feel it; therefore, they can't mature emotionally because they choose to escape instead of mature.

Lastly, they also stop maturing morally. This is important! If your prodigal started their addiction in their teens, it is quite possible they morally react like an adolescent. For instance, they don't think in moral absolutes like "thou shall not;" they don't see wrong as an absolute that God has established.

Instead, they will reason more like an adolescent: "If Mommy catches me, it's wrong, but if nobody knows, it's not wrong." What does this look like? Imagine the crazy conversation that would ensue if you caught your teen smoking pot in their bedroom, and they react in anger because you were in their room.

Addictions rob people of natural progression in these life-developing areas, and that is why a prodigal can be fifty or sixty years old and act like a teenager. It is possible that you are unknowingly dealing with not only your child but your prodigal's addition-generated behavior. And this could be part of the reason for the irrational conversations and the behavior and choices your prodigal keeps making. This is why I want you to understand what an addiction is because this knowledge can help you to understand your prodigal.

"

ADDICTIONS ROB PEOPLE OF NATURAL PROGRESSION IN THESE LIFE-DEVELOPING AREAS

Now, not all prodigals have addictions, but in my experience, many prodigals do create addictions as a result of rejecting the Father. As such, it is important that we understand the nine familiar characteristics of addiction and do in simple terms. These characteristics can apply to substances or behaviors. As you read through each characteristic, do your best to assess if your prodigal has an active addiction in their life. Of course, you might not know the answer to some of these, depending on your current relationship with your prodigal and how good they are at hiding.

They tried to stop and failed

Trying to stop usually happens early on, but there can be multiple repeat cycles of trying to stop (a behavior or substance use) and failing. The addict has moments of clarity and says to themselves, "I have got to stop this!" "I can't keep doing this!" "This isn't getting me anywhere." They try to stop cold turkey or even set up a strategy to quit, but then they fall once again.

Make promises to stop the behavior and failed

These usually are not just promises to themselves, but to their spouse, employer, family member, business partner, or probation officer. Those who make these promises usually will do so clearly and emphatically, declaring, "I'm not going to do that again. I promise!" Then they go right back to the behavior, failing to stop. This can also be cyclical in that they promise again and again and get caught again and again.

They have consequences

Like any bad choice, over time, the addiction intersects with reality. The addict, because they create and reinforce in their minds that there are no rules or that they make the rules and that there are no consequences, are truly surprised when a natural consequence arrives. For instance, this could be a warning at their job or loss of a job, loss of a friend or romantic relationship, or marital separation or divorce. They could have an accident or health consequences due to their addiction. Their financial situation could be in crisis. The list is endless, but consequences for their choices occur in the addict's life.

Keep using after consequences

The addict can have a consequence, even a significant one, and still use. I remember my step-father had lung cancer, had his throat removed, and had to talk through a device, and still smoked. The addict will often keep using even after several consequences occur in their life.

They do more and more

Addicts are not the occasional user. They don't gamble on just one sporting event a year; the behavior may start small and occur infrequently, but then over time, the regularity becomes more and more, often progressing over time from several times a week to several times a day. If you see more and more of the behavior or substance creeping in, this definitely is a sign of a growing addiction.

It takes more for the high or escape

When someone starts an addiction, it's typically in small doses of the substance or the behavior. This small dose supplies enough for the person to get a high or make their escape. Over time they build a tolerance to that dosage of substance or the behavior, so it takes more and more to get the same effect.

More time

As the addict goes down the road of addiction, the amount of time they engage with addictive behavior increases. A person starting off with an occasional pornography engagement can progress to an hour, then multiple hours a week. This could apply to substances as well. The addict takes more time seeking out the behavior, participating in the behaviors, and recovering from the behavior as time goes on.

Withdrawals

This may or may not be something as a parent you would be able to spot; however, when an addict can't get access to their behavior or substance, they can get more anxious, moody, irritable, and irrational. You might experience this on vacations if they haven't brought a supply with them. If they are into hard drugs, this can show up in shakes and other physical symptoms.

Less time for other activities or relationships

As the addict moves down the path of addiction, they not only require more time for the addictive behavior, but they also begin to isolate themselves. They have less time for hobbies, sports, working out, or whatever activities they were involved in prior to the addiction. This is also true of friendships and family relationships that don't participate in or support the addictive behavior.

Now, let me put this list altogether, so you can look at it all at one time:

1. They tried to stop and failed
2. Made promises to stop the behavior and failed
3. They have consequences
4. Keep using after consequences
5. They do more and more
6. It takes more for the high/escape
7. More time
8. Withdrawals
9. Less time for other activities/relationships

As you think of your child while reading these nine characteristics of addiction, does he or she have three or more of these characteristics as it relates to a substance or behavior? If the answer is yes, your prodigal may have created one or multiple addictions in their life.

The addiction is sometimes what brings them to a breaking point where they seek help, be it treatment, counseling, or 12 step groups. For some prodigals this might also be their first step toward coming back to their senses and returning to God.

The prodigal could also whole-heartedly repent, come back to God, and may still have to address the addiction issues. I find, if a prodigal believes they need help to address these issues, it is best to support their desire for recovery than to oppose or denying that they may need assistance.

Now, as a psychologist, I want to share something with you. As a parent, you were likely all-in with your children. You poured your heart, time, and resources into your child. You did not expect all the heartache this prodigal has caused you, your spouse, or your other children; your pain is biting, raw, and at times overwhelming. Combined with the years of struggle, this could become one of the most painful times of your life.

When a soul is in such deep pain for so long, as is sometimes the case for a parent with a prodigal child, one could seek comfort in a substance or behavior to medicate the pain. I've seen parents turn to food, shopping, social media, prescription drugs, glasses of wine, or overusing a cell phone. Examine your behavior or substance use and see if you have three or more of the characteristics of addiction; if you think you are moving down a path of addiction as a means of coping with the pain, as compassionately and firmly as I can say it in love, get help! People do not overcome addictions by themselves. I recommend starting with a Christian counselor with whom you can be honest and receive accountability. If you need a support group, don't let pride stop you from healing.

"

PEOPLE DO NOT OVERCOME ADDICTIONS BY THEMSELVES.

If there is an addiction in the marriage, both people in the marriage and all the family members are impacted. You and all those you love deserve the best of you!

CHAPTER
Five
SECRET TRAUMA

In this chapter, we are going to travel into probably the most sacred and possibly the most shameful or injured part of your prodigal. This is not a place many parents visit or are invited into. The area I want to walk through is your prodigal's sexuality and its potential connection to them going down the path of a prodigal.

Now, I want you to read this chapter all the way through. I know no parent wants to think about, believe or embrace the potential sexual traumas or experiences that their child has had. I cannot tell you how many prodigals that were fifty to seventy-five years old at the time I saw them, and I was the first one with whom they shared their sexual trauma, rape, or abortion. The pain, secrecy, and lies they told themselves and believed for decades, had a considerable influence on their decision to walk away from God and their family. I know as Christians, we might feel that this couldn't happen; however, it does! I have had many Christian adult clients who have not only experienced sexual trauma but have experienced it in their own home, the home of another Christian family, church buildings and retreat centers, and Christian camps. I don't say this to shame you but rather to inform you: many good Christian parents have children who have experienced sexual trauma.

Now, not all of these children and teens become prodigals, but if they make a decision to pull away, it could be directly related to an experience they have never told you or anyone else. This deep lurking secret gnaws at their soul and feeds them lies that it was their fault or that they are now worthless because they are not virgins.

This can be true whether your child is male or female. One in three females will experience sexual abuse before the age of eighteen. That means 30 percent of the women in your church have been sexually abused or raped. Additionally, males by the age of eighteen will experience sexual trauma at about half the rate of females. This means one in six males will experience some type of sexual trauma, so we could say in any given church, about 15 percent of males have experienced sexual trauma.

Now, when I talk about sexual trauma, the types can vary significantly. For instance, they could be exposed to pornography, which can cause them shame and give them a secret to keep. This trauma could be compounded if the incident was at the hands of a parent or family member. Another example is they could have been fondled or asked to fondle or even have been asked to give or receive oral stimulation. You see, sexual abuse can include anything from an inappropriate conversation and touch to actual penetration in any manner. These behaviors could be perpetrated by someone of the opposite sex, same-sex, a peer, an adult in authority, a friend, family member, or stranger. This abuse could have been a one-time act or happen multiple times, or even by various people during different incidents.

Imagine a young soul having such a secret. They often blame themselves—especially if they are too young to have abstract reasoning—for what happened. They feel dirty, self-disgusted, rejected, used, and alone. They might even have been threatened to keep the secret, and with all this, they still needed to get up the next day and go to school, church on Sunday, and "pretend" nothing was wrong. Depending on how they reflect on the sexual trauma, they might be mad at or question God. Why did you let this happen? Why didn't you protect me? Do you really love me? There are all sorts of internal spiritual questions that those who are traumatized don't say out loud. These thoughts and feelings go on day-after-day, often for years. This might be the very pain they medicate with addictive behaviors.

> THE PRODIGAL'S FEELINGS OF WORTHLESSNESS AND BEING UNLOVABLE CAN CREATE RELATIONSHIP PATTERNS OF PUSHING HEALTHY AND GOOD RELATIONSHIPS AWAY.

The prodigal's feelings of worthlessness and being unlovable can create relationship patterns of pushing healthy and good relationships away and drawing near to people who share the same worthless and unlovable message inside of them. This may also be why they so fiercely attach to the wrong crowd.

The soul that has been sexually abused can have an enormous internal switch that, if unaddressed, can make this soul's journey very hard to heal and more prone to self-medication. When trauma occurs, it can overwhelm the entire system and create what I call a trauma reset in my book *Partner Betrayal Trauma*. A trauma reset takes a soul back to the first stage of development. In this first stage of human development, the soul must figure out whether to trust or mistrust its environment and the people involved in its development.

"

WHEN TRAUMA OCCURS, IT CAN OVERWHELM THE ENTIRE SYSTEM AND CREATE WHAT I CALL A TRAUMA RESET.

As Christian parents, you were most likely trustworthy and created a safe environment; however, sexual trauma can take that safe soul back to that heart decision and cause the person to redefine their environment and the people in it as being unsafe, and thus cannot be trusted. If the soul makes this conclusion, they go down the rest of the stages of human development created by Erik Erikson. This by itself could lead to years of choices that are not in their best interest.

There could be endless repercussions for someone who has experienced sexual trauma. If your prodigal has experienced this kind of trauma, this will most likely be the deepest, darkest secret that they are carrying. Your child could experience depression, challenges at school, loss of interest in regular social activities, gain or lose significant weight, or over compensate by seeking to be a perfectionist. This child could experience suicidal thoughts or attempt to take their life. And, if the perpetrator threatened to kill parents or made other appalling threats, the child could feel a double burden to keep the secret. Sexual trauma and keeping it secret could be the single reason why a prodigal has such a radical change in behaviors and beliefs. This experience will also be part of the journey in deciding to make or keep God as first in their lives.

I have asked prodigals if they were sexually abused. Depending on the circumstances, person, or how they have blamed themselves, they might answer no. However, I have met hundreds of men who were sexually abused by an eighteen-year-old or older female when they were thirteen or so, and they never understood that it was both sexual abuse and a felony. Now, I have learned to and trained therapists around the world to ask a better question: "How old were you for your first sexual encounter of any kind? And how old was the other person?" I have found that asking clients these questions helps me assess whether it was sexual abuse. If sexual abuse is part of their history, I strongly recommend finding a Christian counselor who has specialty training in treating sexual trauma.

Rape is another sexual trauma that can happen to either gender at any age. Rape will have all of the impacts of sexual trauma because it is another form of sexual trauma. As prodigals make poor choices and associate with people who make poor choices, rape could easily occur under the influence of drugs and alcohol. If your prodigal has been raped, this will also need to be address pre-or-post coming back to Christ. Again, I strongly recommend a Christian counselor.

I know and acknowledge that what we are covering is very heavy and something you hope has never happened to your child. However, in my clinical experience, once a soul opens up and shares its sexual secrets, it can heal much more fully. They can start destroying the lies they told themselves and begin to feel loveable and worthy again. They can begin to view themselves as being worth, just as God says they are.

Before I leave this subject of sexual trauma, I need to share one last potentially deep dark secret that your prodigal may be carrying deep in their soul: reckless sexuality. The chances of your prodigal having had sex are high. They may even have had or still have unprotected sex. And while unprotected sex is often, and appropriately so, associated with sexually transmitted disease, that is not the secret I am alluding to. I want to discuss a trauma that can go deep into the heart and body of a prodigal—the secret of having had or being responsible for an abortion.

When raised in a Christian home, prodigals comprehend their parents' values and the basic teachings of their church on moral issues. And getting pregnant outside of marriage is definitely one of the known behaviors that is believed to outside of those values. But now, they are pregnant.

I have learned from women who have had an abortion that it is a full-body experience. She walks shamefully into a clinic, strips off her clothes, puts on a surgical gown, and is aware of what is going to happen. Even if she is sedated, her body fully experiences this trauma. When she wakes up, she is different. She has experienced trauma! She may have broken something so deep and sacred in her that she not only doesn't trust others, she no longer trusts herself. She may truly reject herself and believe she is unlovable and unforgivable. And some female prodigals have gone through multiple abortions—each one as traumatic as the one before. This is a secret they often vow to tell no one, especially their parents.

Men don't escape the trauma of participating in abortion, even if the woman gave them no option. I can attest that as men heal from the loss of a child through abortion, the trauma is real, the counseling is hard, and the tears are many.

As a prodigal, this is rarely a question anyone ever asks them. For some, this is at the core of rejecting God because they believe He would reject them. Even with this, they can heal from abortion! I have seen it many times; however, this is a real issue pre-and-post coming back to Christ. And, as with all sexual traumas, this most likely needs professional help to heal from.

Thinking about your child's sexuality is understandably uncomfortable. It may have stirred fears or memories you don't want to think about; however, doing so is very important. I am taking my time walking through several aspects of the potential path your prodigal could be on as they choose to reject God, and sexual trauma is often involved.

66

NO TRAUMA IS YOUR FAULT UNLESS YOU DIRECTLY CAUSED THE TRAUMA.

Again, no sexual choice is about you or your parenting. No trauma is your fault unless you directly caused the trauma. The prodigal journey is not a simple process for a person to understand. There are different variables and experiences, and relationship choices that come into play. I find as a parent learns about each of these dynamics, they can be more understanding and maybe even more compassionate toward their prodigal and how they chose their path. They can also put less emphasis on their parenting and the risk of assuming false blame for why their child is a prodigal.

CHAPTER

Six

SEX

In the previous chapter, I shared about sexual trauma. In this chapter, I will share about sex in general. The purpose of this chapter is to help you understand another possible element of your prodigal's journey that, unless you are a sex researcher, you would not understand. I find this piece of information may answer some of the questions you might have as to "What do they see in that person?" "Why are they staying with that person?" and "Why are they so protective of that romantic relationship that they know I don't approve of?"

We already know most prodigals who choose to reject God, regardless of their parenting, go down a path that, in many cases, involves sex with others. Why is this such a big deal? Why is sex by itself such a powerful issue for the prodigal to work through before and after coming back to Christ?

I want to take you on a side trip from my own life. I was a prodigal, and my story includes sexual immorality. I got radically saved, but early on still struggled. Then, growing in my relationship with Christ, I was in Bible school, and one day I was reading the scripture, and I had one of the WHA-MO experiences. I was reading 1 Corinthians 6:18: "Flee from sexual immorality. All other sins a person commits are outside the body, but whoever sins sexually, sins against their own body." I was so excited about this scripture because I was discovering that sexual sin was somehow different than lying or stealing or most of the ten commandments; sexual sin had something to do with the body.

Now, I have to set the stage a little bit so you understand where in my story this revelation happened. As I mentioned, I was in Bible school, and it was the early 1980's. We didn't have computers (imagine that) or cell phones, and all research had to be done in this place called the library. Not wanting to delay getting an answer to my question, I went to my Bible school professors and asked them to clarify the meaning of the verse and to explain how sexual sin is different. Again and again, they all gave the same answer: all sins are the same. I graduated from Bible school without receiving a satisfactory answer to my question.

Then I attended the world's largest protestant seminary (at the time). We had some of the best Bible scholars; I asked my new professors the same questions: "How is sexual sin different, and how is it connected to the body?" Alas, my question was never answered during my education.

While working on my master's degree, I started counseling people who were addicted to sex. To learn more, I began reading about the very new field of neuroscience where researchers were discovering how the brain actually works, what impacts the brain, and how to measure impact on the brain. I signed up for their journal reviews, and finally, I found my answer to my biblical questions. You see, they were in the early stages of studying how sex impacts the brain and how powerful sex is to the brain.

I want to share with you in an abbreviated manner what neuroscience has brought to light about our amazing sexual design by our Creator. This information can help you better understand not only the spiritual and emotional battle your prodigal might be waging but also the physiological battle they have to overcome to stop a sexual relationship, whether it is a person, fantasy, or pornography.

The first thing that the neuroscience community discovered is the powerful connection between sex and the brain (again, how God created us). When a person has an orgasm, the brain receives the highest level of endogenous opiates sent to the pleasure center of the brain. Endogenous opiates provide your brain with a heroin-like substance, and this pleasure drug is received with incredible intensity to your brain. Since you are likely a parent, I will assume you have had an orgasm. That orgasm, neurologically speaking, is the absolute highest form of pleasure that your brain can create and receive, without exception.

The second thing neuroscience has shown us about the brain and sex is equally amazing. When we have this orgasm, whatever we are looking at, real or imaginary, we literally attach to it. THIS IS HUGE!

And lastly, when you have an orgasm toward a picture, person, or fantasy, you create a desire to repeat that attachment to this person, picture, or fantasy. Your brain literally wants to do it again with this picture, person, or fantasy.

Let me take you back to high school or college psychology class for a moment. Remember a man called Pavlov who created a saliva response in a dog by ringing a bell before feeding him? Pavlov's dog was the basis for what is now called classical conditioning—ring the bell, feed the dog. Now, let's apply this to sex. You have a sexual stimulus, be it a real person, a fantasy, or pornography, and you engage sexually to the point of orgasm, and like a spider's web, these chemicals attach you to this person, picture, or fantasy just as Pavlov's dog attached himself to the ringing bell.

Now, consider this in light of the behavior of a prodigal as they repeatedly attach to a person. Regardless of what type, size, gender, or belief system they might have, they will neurologically, as well as spiritually and emotionally, become attached. You know this is true if you have been in a long-term monogamous relationship with your spouse; you grow more and more attached over the years, and they become more and more desirable to you.

So, here was my long-awaited answer to "whoever sins sexually, sins against their own body" (1 Corinthians 6:18). Because we are sexual beings, we want to repeat sexual encounters again and again. The more we do, the more our bodies gain stronger and stronger attachment to that fantasy, picture, or person. This means, not only is your prodigal "becoming one" with whoever or whatever they are having sex with, they are creating a desire within themselves to seek out the highest chemical reward the body has: the desire to reconnect. And this doesn't even take into account the spiritual and emotional part of attaching.

So, you see, if a person makes a choice to leave a sexual relationship, they are fighting against their own body. If this happens, they would probably go through withdrawals spiritually, emotionally, and physiologically. Also, as a parent of a prodigal, it is possible that you don't know that your prodigal is connecting and reconnecting with lust, pornography, and the attachment that comes with an orgasm and how this too can make them seek out people who find their immoral behaviors acceptable.

I tell you all this to help you understand why it is a challenge for prodigals (or anyone with a sexual addiction) to make the right choice. It may be clear that the choice they are making is the wrong one and that it is against what God tells us not to do. But if the wrong choice has been made again and again, and an attachment has been created, change is extraordinarily difficult. And to be fair, your prodigal also doesn't know the neuroscience behind sexual attachment. This attachment is why they want to stay or defend a sexual relationship they are currently in, regardless of your opinions or their own. They are not questioning their growing attachment either, often because it feels like they are more and more in love.

When having relationship issues with your prodigal, this understanding of how the brain works may help you recognize the reason why they are so often in an impassioned state of protecting the emotional and physiological rewards of the relationship and why you cannot logically reason with them. When having conversations about their relationship, you may want to question whether to have them or not, knowing their attachment with your prodigal. Understanding that your prodigal is bonded chemically to this other person, and not you, is important. Overplaying your hand here can injure your relationship with the prodigal. They already know what you believe about their relationship. In fact, they could possibly write out nearly verbatim what you would say to them, so trust me, your message is already inside them. Also, let's not forget the Holy Spirit. It is He who will continue to convict your son or daughter of their sin without any need of your assistance.

"

UNDERSTANDING THAT YOUR PRODIGAL IS BONDED CHEMICALLY TO THIS OTHER PERSON, AND NOT YOU, IS IMPORTANT.

When our children were young, like many children, they wanted a dog. I didn't want a dog. I grew up with dogs and remembered the work more than the good times; however, never pit yourself against the prayers of a little girl. So, my wife said if we got a dog, it would have to be a blond Afghan Hound (we had two before we had children). And guess what? She found one on the internet, and you could tell this puppy had the gentlest heart. We called him Moses, and we learned as he grew and matured, Moses was stunningly handsome and truly as gentle as a dog could be.

One day when Moses was a few years old, I grilled some monstrous T-bone steaks. We rarely treated him to real food, but I thought, "Why not give the dog a bone like I did when growing up?" So, I did. And as you can imagine, he was committed to that bone. I then wanted to move him from where he was eating that bone to another spot. As I reached out to take Moses' bone away from him, he growled and tried to bite me. He was serious about protecting that bone. I realized at that moment this gentle giant of a dog, which I fed, groomed, walked, and loved for years, was a different animal when I was trying to take away something he didn't want to keep.

Why did I tell you this story? I am sure you know.

The child you poured yourself into is attached to that person just as Moses was committed to his bone. If your prodigal thinks you are trying to take his "bone" away, so to speak, they could turn on you. Yes, irrationally, not able to see the big picture or even that your concerns are valid, they will "growl" at you and "show their teeth" to tell you to back off. If this is the response you are getting, you might decide the method you are using isn't working, and as Jesus has revealed to us, you might decide to use a different tact—to love your prodigal, even though their choices are poor.

Remember, life is a movie, not a photograph. This means your prodigal is a certain way at a certain time—a photograph. They can at any time "come to their senses," and the movie can turn out to be one in which God gets the glory of returning another prodigal home and using their story to help others.

I hope that this conversation on the power of sex and how it can be a huge influence in your prodigal's life, is both helpful and gives you wisdom as you walk through each photograph of your prodigal's movie.

CHAPTER

Seven

DISORDERS

This chapter will not necessarily relate to everyone; however, if this is the case for you, I encourage you to read this for the future. Some of you might know other parents of prodigals or even lead a parent group in your church or home, and this information might be what they need to understand their prodigal's situation.

As I have said throughout, I am a Christian psychologist. Christian is first because Jesus is my Lord and Savior, and the Word of God is the final authority for living life in time. As a counselor then psychologist, I have had to learn a lot about the soul, much like a plumber has to learn about plumbing.

In our field, we use the word disorder to explain how the soul or body has maladapted to its circumstances in life. I believe outside of chemical disorders (I'll explain in a minute) that psychological disorders are a person's effort to adapt to survive the harshness, coldness, or uncertainty of its circumstances, including that of their family.

Psychological disorders exist on a continuum where on the left there are no disorders, on the right, there is a disorder, and in the middle of the continuum are what we call "features." Features of a disorder means this is the direction the soul is morphing or adapting toward. For example, if "X" disorder had to have five yes answers, they only have three. This would tell me we need to get to work, or things will get worse.

When someone has a diagnosable disorder, they have measurably arrived at an adaptation. In other words, if disorder "X" needs five yes answers, they have positively answered five or more questions that qualify them for "X" disorder.

"

WHEN SOMEONE HAS A DIAGNOSABLE DISORDER, THEY HAVE MEASURABLY ARRIVED AT AN ADAPTATION.

I have seen and believe in the complete neuro-plasticity of the human soul. We, through sin, can change; and through observing God's Word, we can change. I have seen many people diagnosed with a disorder, and a year or two later, not one characteristic remained. As humans, we have a will and, with that, the ability to choose to grow, adapt, or stay the same. A diagnosis is a snapshot of where someone is at that moment in time; it is not a life sentence unless that person chooses it.

As I briefly identify a variety of disorders, I want to caution you from diagnosing anyone. A diagnosis is given _only_ after the person has taken a psychological test such as an MMPI with a licensed psychologist. A counselor who listens to your story and says the prodigal's diagnosis is "X" could be doing you a disservice. This is why I tell you this.

I recently had a case when a counselor allowed a husband and wife to use undiagnosed names for each other. They participated in a counseling intensive with me—a 5-day session— which includes a psychological assessment (Minnesota Multiphasic Personality Inventory [MMPI]), and neither of them had the claimed diagnosis. Again _only_ a licensed psychologist, after a proper assessment, should give someone a legitimate diagnosis.

The only reason I am sharing some of these diagnoses is that if you are dealing with one of them and it is not addressed, the prodigal's life can be harder, and it could prolong the journey back home or make it harder even after returning to God. If you recognize any of the features as being present in your child, please pursue additional legitimate research on the topic. If you Google "DSM" (short for Diagnostic and Statistical Manual of Mental Disorders) and "diagnosis," you will come up with better information. Please avoid blogs by well-meaning people with no clinical background as they are prone to provide anecdotes and experiences rather than medical counsel and are more likely to have misinformation than would clinical sources.

CHEMICAL/PERSONALITY DISORDERS

Earlier I discussed the field of neuroscience and the study of the brain. This field has helped bring clarity for those with chemical disorders. A chemical disorder, unless induced by chemical abuse, is generally believed to be more genetically based. The prodigal didn't ask for their brain to have certain chemical imbalances or dysfunctions.

Suppose a prodigal exhibits behavior consistent with that of a known disorder? If the person is a client of mine, before suggesting they see a psychiatrist, I will refer them to be evaluated at one of Dr. Amen's clinics located across the nation. Why? Dr. Amen's clinics evaluate the brain in several different ways over a couple of days, giving the client a multi-page report at the end with a specific action plan. In contrast, a psychiatrist can only guess the type of medicine and action plan needed. I have not had one client dissatisfied with their results from their time with the clinics.

BIPOLAR

In the bipolar family of disorders, the mildest form is cyclothymia. This disorder causes minor up and down mood instability. In my experience, the person who has this disorder feels like they have a funky day, but when they track it, day-to-day and week-to-week, it's almost predictable.

Bipolar I and II are mood swings that are not connected to direct circumstances. The person can get up with pressured speech which is the tendency to speak rapidly and frenziedly, then down in energy, not motivated, and could even feel depressed. In bipolar, the person usually is going up and down for days at a time. In the manic/depressive state, these ups and downs could occur cyclically for much longer periods of time, with the length of the ups often being equally matched with the lengths of the downs.

Once this person has been diagnosed, they will want to see a psychiatrist for medical management. As a parent, these moods may make no sense and can be drastic.

SCHIZOPHRENIA

Schizophrenia is when a person experiences hallucinations and delusions, and their way of explaining what is going on in their world doesn't make sense. If someone is paranoid schizophrenic, they could develop wild stories such as people being after them. If your prodigal has this diagnosis, it can be chaotic. This would need a management team in place, including a psychiatrist and usually social service help, due to them not being able to function or work. It's important to note here: this is _not_ a result of your parenting.

The above list is not all-inclusive, as there are personality disorders that are not medically based.

DEPRESSION

Depression can be a chemical, hormonal, or psychological imbalance. It is an epidemic in Western society. It is so multifaceted and can be confused with other medical issues. For example, low testosterone in both men and women can look very similar to the symptoms of depression. When a client has symptoms of depression, I first want them to get their thyroid checked because low thyroid has very similar symptoms as depression. I also have them get their hormone panel done. Then I will have a better understanding of what might be wrong.

Depression can be caused by a stage of grief or significant loss, a result of burnout, or by total neglect of self-care. Depression can also be a result of holding in rage from trauma or neglect. You see, depression can come from several angles, so identifying the causes is the precursor to choosing the correct treatment.

The following list includes the general symptoms of depression. If your prodigal is having five or more of these symptoms, depression could be present.

- Low energy
- Difficulty concentrating
- Difficulty making decisions
- Significant weight gain/loss
- Feeling worthless
- Possible suicidal thoughts
- Sleep disturbance
- Not getting pleasure from activities

Depression can also be part of the prodigal parent process. Having a prodigal child can be spiritually and emotionally volatile for moms and dads, and for everyone involved. If you are having five or more of the symptoms listed above, you will want to address this issue as soon as possible.

BORDERLINE DISORDER

Borderline disorders are ones that can create significant chaos for you and your family. A person who has a borderline disorder can make bad choices that have severe consequences, and, unfortunately, they keep repeating this pattern. The borderline's moods can be very unstable. They have challenges with anger outbursts, make suicidal gestures, and are usually impulsive in at least two areas of their life, such as spending, alcohol, and sex.

The borderline tends to get in relationships, which at first are wonderful and amazing, then something happens, and they end up disliking that person. The borderline hates to be rejected but sets it up so they are. They have a challenge with stable care-of-self and can feel empty inside. The best way I have heard a borderline describe this feeling is that it feels like an emotional pinball machine.

NARCISSISM

A narcissist is characterized by grandiosity, self-absorption, manipulation of others, no remorse for impact on others, being entitled, envy, acting superior, and expecting to be acknowledged as superior without the accomplishments to back it up, and they do not handle criticism well.

Many addicts appear narcissistic because of the lack of spiritual, emotional, and moral development we discussed earlier. Prodigals may develop narcissistic tendencies as a result of rejecting God and going down the path of being their own God.

Now, I caution you, if your prodigal has an addiction, they may have some symptoms of narcissism, and if they do, you would want to encourage them to be assessed sometime after recovering from their addictions.

I have a DVD on narcissism and addiction if this is of interest to you. The name of the DVD is *Narcissism: Sex Addiction and Intimacy Anorexia*.

Again, make sure you have this assessed before giving an opinion about it.

SCHIZOID PERSONALITY DISORDER

One way to describe this disorder is the lone-wolf persona. Unlike all the other disorders, rarely is this person in chaos internally or externally. The schizoid personality disorder is someone who has closed themselves off. They tend not to have emotionally close friends—short or long-term. They do not desire sex if they marry, and they don't get pleasure out of activities. If you meet a schizoid, they appear distant or aloof. They are not reactive to praise or criticism, and they live in a type of indifference towards others.

There are other disorders a prodigal can have; however, these are the majority of the ones I have seen in my office. It's important to note that in most cases, you, as a parent, did not cause these to develop. Your prodigal will need to address them after they have been evaluated. And sometimes, upon learning a medical diagnosis, prodigals begin to understand why they keep going around the same mountain again and again.

As a parent, rarely will you be actively involved in treating these disorders. Much like a physical condition, you would let the professionals do their job and be supportive.

My hope is if you are dealing with a disorder, you get informed as much as you can. This will help you acquire tools that can mitigate the impact of the disorder on you and your prodigal while allowing you to still have compassion and healthy boundaries with the soul of your prodigal.

CHAPTER
Eight
TRUST OR MISTRUST

Earlier, I alluded to the issue of trust that prodigals can develop as a result of experiencing trauma. This trust issue is a significant issue; I feel we need to give it some time for you to comprehend it better as it relates to your prodigal.

As a parent of a prodigal and a believer, in many cases, you come at life trusting God, trusting others, and in most cases having a positive outcome. You also generally trust yourself. You tend to make good decisions, and you listen to the Holy Spirit and act on what He is saying if you feel something is off in your life. Experientially you may not have a whole lot of involvement with mistrust, so as we walk through this, understand your prodigal doesn't think, feel, or believe as you do. I believe this can give you more insight into the heart of your prodigal.

The prodigal process, by definition, is not trusting God. The prodigal doesn't trust God as a person. The prodigal doesn't trust God's Word and doesn't believe they will be judged by God. Remember, the first step of being a prodigal is not putting God first and thus developing a thankless spirit.

"

THE PRODIGAL DOESN'T TRUST GOD'S WORD AND DOESN'T BELIEVE THEY WILL BE JUDGED BY GOD.

Dr. Erik Erikson's model of human development can help us to understand where the prodigal might be in the process of walking down the road of trust or mistrust. I'm sharing this because most of the prodigals I have worked with have had trust issues. I can't tell you how many times I have heard, "Doc, I don't trust anyone." When they say this, they can mean God, their spouse, boss, neighbors, and even themselves. Their mistrust is not a statement about you at all. The mistrust is universal and, as stated, is often internal as well as external.

I am going to walk through the positive side of Dr. Erikson's model of human development created in the 1950s. His work is broadly accepted and presents eight stages of human development progressing from birth to old age.

Stage One: Trust

This is the first task for a successful human to develop. Infants, well before they are able to speak, evaluate whether they can trust that their needs will be met. They assess their caretaker's consistency in feeding, talking to them, eye contact, and touch, as all are significant. If babies conclude they are safe, they decide to trust. Thereafter, all subsequent stages of human development are built on a foundation of trust.

Stage Two: Autonomy

Stage two happens when the child starts distinguishing that they are separate beings from their caretakers. They can sense their thoughts and perceptions as separate from what is going on around them.

Stage Three: Initiative

In this stage, the child begins to see cause and effect. They can squeeze a toy, and it squeaks. They can laugh, and you laugh. They observe that what they do has some impact on their environment and relationships.

Stage Four: Industry

In this stage, the child/person comes to believe "I can." They begin to develop a sense of trust in themselves and that they are generally capable.

Stage Five: Identity

In this stage of life, the person is getting a handle on their strengths, as well as who they are in the world.

Stage Six: Intimacy

The soul is secure in itself and in its relationships. The soul is able to give itself to others, including strong romantic relationships.

Stage Seven: Generosity

In this stage of life, you have accomplished things. Your life becomes more about giving back to others in service, resources, or in the ways you believe make a difference in the lives of others.

Stage Eight: Integrity

This happens when you have lived life well. You are pleased with the fruits of your labor and pleased with the legacy you are leaving your family and others.

> "
> A PRODIGAL CAN SHIFT FROM MISTRUST TO TRUST
> AND GAIN ALL THE BENEFITS IF THEY SO CHOOSE.

For those who were able to grow up this way, or like myself, were able to be re-taught by the Holy Spirit by the renewing of our minds (see Romans 12:1-2), our lives get brighter and brighter with age. I write this to give you hope that a prodigal can shift from mistrust to trust and gain all the benefits if they so choose.

Now, let me walk you through the same stages of human development if a soul starts to and continues in mistrust. This is often the path of the prodigal. As a prodigal mistrusts God, makes poor choices, and distrusts self and others, there is a known path ahead for them. This information can give you another lens through which you can discover the depths of your prodigal. Again, my hope is that awareness and information can help you have compassion on the soul, as well as awareness of a process.

Stage One: Mistrust

The heart of an infant or growing/grown person concludes, "I am not safe" "It is not safe out there." "I can't trust others to meet my needs." This mistrust becomes the foundation of most of the prodigal's reasoning. They will accuse you and others of being controlling, which is a way to say loudly and clearly, "I don't trust." For the prodigal, it is universal—they don't trust God, themselves, or others.

Stage Two: Shame

Here the soul concludes, "I am bad." This is not the same as bad things happen; this is "I am the bad thing." This can lead to self-loathing, lower self-esteem, and not feeling worthy of good.

Stage Three: Guilt

Here the prodigal will withdraw from godly and healthy relationships. You can see the progression, such as, "I don't trust others." "I don't measure up." "I am bad." "I don't know who I am." If these are your internal messages, you don't want to be around someone who knows God, themselves, and why they are here.

Stage Four: Inferiority

Here the soul measures itself against others and determines it is lacking. The message it starts to believe is, "I am less than others." "I can't." Once a person believes these lies and adopts them as their core thoughts, it can affect every area of their life.

Stage Five: Confusion

Here the prodigal doesn't know who they are. Typically, we learn this from God during our lives—who we are and why we are here—but since the prodigal avoids God, they lack a sense of who they are and most likely their purpose.

Stage Six: Isolation

Here the prodigal will definitely withdraw from godly and healthy relationships. You can clearly see the progression, such as, "I don't trust others." "I don't measure up." "I am bad." "I don't know who

I am." If these are your internal messages, you don't want to be around someone who knows God, themselves, and why they are here.

Stage Seven: Stagnation

Regardless of the age of the prodigal, they seem stuck, and their life is not going anywhere. At best, they are marking time. They appear to be living in a fog, not able to see or prepare for a future.

Stage Eight: Despair

The last stage of going down the road the prodigal is traveling is despair. The soul looks over the decades of poor choices, broken relationships, poor planning, and deep inside, they feel despair or regret. They have little perspective of legacy, and they feel the sadness of life frittering away.

Now, imagine having all these horrible thoughts, feelings, and beliefs about yourself rolling around your heart on a daily basis: you don't trust; you don't feel good about yourself; you're confused; going nowhere and overwhelmed. This soul regularly stays hurt and offended. It feels judged, ashamed, and frustrated. This heart doesn't like itself or the reality it has created.

I tell you this so when your prodigal does some of the things they do; you might be able to see that they don't trust or feel good about themselves, or they may even feel unworthy of any good in their life. They're not trusting themselves, and this judgement of themselves can keep them on this known developmental path. As a parent, this can be heartbreaking.

I remember one week I had two extreme cases of, "Doc, I don't trust anyone."

First was a woman who was raped at fourteen. Up to that point in her life, she had what she considered an ideal life, but as rape can do, it caused a trauma reset that she had to mend after she found out about her husband's affair.

The second person was a man who had a terrible event happen to him early in childhood and was abandoned. He, too, did not trust anyone.

That week I explained to both clients how trauma could reset you to mistrust. They both read a very basic outline of Dr. Erickson's model. Once they read the trust and mistrust sides of how we develop, they both had exactly the same response, "That is me straight down the line."

Learning the model enabled them to see their choice to mistrust had a known path of consequences. In fact, each asked a similar follow-up question: "How do I fix it?" My suggestion was for them to attend a support group which can help build the steps to trust. They did, and both regained trust in God, self, and others.

For some prodigals, like the one we read about in the prodigal son parable Jesus told, a prodigal needs to experience a massive crisis in order for them to hit bottom. At the bottom, they will have to trust others to feed them, give them a place to stay, a job, and encouragement. I tell you this because any progress, even slow progress, is a good thing. Again, you most likely didn't cause this trust issue. The prodigal often chooses not to trust while in adolescence, and this includes trust in God. Remember. Your child being a prodigal is not a result of your parenting; it is an active and ongoing choice not to let God be God in their lives, even if the trust was broken by you.

"

ANY PROGRESS, EVEN SLOW PROGRESS, IS A GOOD THING.

With this, I encourage you to pray that God will give them experiences to trust. You can pray that their heart could become open to trusting.

Now, don't go and try to make them trust you. Trust is an inside job. The issue isn't that you are trustworthy; the issue is their heart has to learn trust.

"

A PRODIGAL CAN HEAL AND HAVE A GREAT LIFE.

Now, I hope, as you continue to grow in your understanding of the internal process of their journey, you can continue to let go of any false responsibility you have assigned to yourself or your spouse. Remember, prodigals can learn to trust and love and receive love. A prodigal can heal and have a great life. You might see them and yourself in the photograph but believe in the movie.

CHAPTER
Nine
THE WILL

When God created all of us, including your prodigal, He gave us a gift none in heaven has. When God created Adam, His first words to him were, "You are free." Prior to this, never in all of God's timelessness were these three words spoken.

God knew when He gave this gift to mankind, mankind would have authority over themselves in time and that this would impact the location of their eternal soul. With the risk that only some of us would love and serve Him freely, He created the free will children called humans.

This human will is one of the most powerful forces on earth. This human will has created amazing structures on the earth and medicines that do amazing tasks. This human will has created incredible technologies that are incomprehensible to many of us. But, even with all this good, this human will has also raped, destroyed, created wars, and wiped out whole civilizations. This human will has asserted itself above God; it's created thousands of false gods and reaped severe consequences for rebelling against the Father that created them.

> **THIS HUMAN WILL IS ONE OF THE MOST POWERFUL FORCES ON EARTH.**

When God birthed mankind, He knew He was taking a risk; however, He gave the responsibility of the risk and outcome to the human and not to Himself as a "parent." God relinquished Himself of any responsibility for the choices humans made. Fortunately, because of His grace and love, He gave us Christ to pay for all of our sins and poor use of our will. Even then, He gives us free will to believe what Christ has done and to follow Him.

Now, let's go back in time. Remember when your prodigal was born. As a parent, we remember every child's birth. I remember holding both of my children when they were first born. Like you, I prayed for them and myself as we started this journey of life together.

I remember privately and publicly dedicating them to Christ, hoping that they would follow the ways of our Master, Christ. All who are believers desire and wish this for each child that is born to us in this free will experiment of God's; however, as they are growing up, we realize that they are not us. As I wrote earlier about individualizing and realizing they are them, and not us, I think as parents, we also individuate and realize they are them, and not us. They have their own mind, will, emotions, and gifts. They were placed in a different time and generation than us. They were given a different calling from God than our own. They are not us—they are them! They come completely different. They have a different spirit, sexuality, preferences, desires, and dreams. Deep in our hearts, we know, like the Father, we have participated in birthing a child that may choose to love and honor us and our beliefs, or they may choose to rebel against our hearts and what we believe.

Free will is a powerful thing, and from their first "no" until now, we know that their will is theirs. We as parent know that this will is capable of great good and great harm for themselves and others. This free will God gave you and your child is their birthright, and they are responsible for how they choose to use their will toward God, you, and others in the world. I know, or at least believe you know this, and have learned this lesson repeatedly from all your children—you can't make them do anything. If they choose to obey your ways, that is about who they are. If they choose not to obey your ways, that too is about who they are.

"

SOMEHOW, WE AS PARENTS CAN GET DECEIVED INTO THINKING THAT THEIR CHOICES ARE ABOUT WHO WE ARE.

Somehow, we as parents can get deceived into thinking that their choices are about who we are. Yes, we provide a context, we might even influence, but bottom line, it comes down to them, their choice, and exercising their free will. Accepting how powerless we are as parents when it comes to free choice is important, especially when you are a parent of a prodigal.

Honestly, as a counselor, there is a direct correlation between how powerful you believe you are in your prodigal's life and the pain you will experience for them being a prodigal. The parent that is like God, and gives the free will choices to the child and accepts their powerlessness has incredibly less pain in the prodigal parent process. This parent still hurts and loves, but just doesn't believe in their heart they had anything to do with the choices their child has made or is making.

"

GOD DOESN'T TAKE ANY BLAME OR RESPONSIBILITY FOR THE CHOICES YOUR PRODIGAL HAS MADE.

Remember, the prodigal process is between God and your child. God doesn't take <u>ANY</u> blame or responsibility for the choices your prodigal has made. Remember, He has given them reasonable health, wealth, opportunity, family, church, and so much more for them to make better choices. Plus, He has the benefit and comfort that the Holy Spirit has had many moments and conversations with your child that you may know nothing about.

I will keep saying this throughout the chapter—as a parent, you are NOT the problem, and sadly, you are also NOT the solution. I will dedicate a whole chapter later on this idea.

> ❝
> YOU ARE NOT THE PROBLEM, AND SADLY, YOU ARE ALSO NOT THE SOLUTION.

You might feel like you're the problem, especially if your prodigal blames you for being this or that, for not having enough of this or that. Other children have experienced less from their parents or have maybe even never met their parents, but haven't rejected God.

You might feel like the problem because your prodigal has scapegoated you. In the Old Testament, they would take an animal and put all the sins of the people on that animal and kill it; this where the term scapegoating comes from. Your prodigal may "scapegoat" you because their life is going nowhere, or they are not able to make it or can't figure out who they are.

By now, you should understand, this could be because of an addiction stunting their development or from not trusting. Again, this is not about you. They may want you to feel it's about you, so they don't have to look into the mirror and take responsibility, but don't buy that lie.

One thing I have definitely learned sitting in my counseling chair these several decades is if someone doesn't want to take responsibility, they want to give it to someone else.

Your prodigal might even try to manipulate you out of false guilt so that you might feel shame. I tell my clients that feelings are not facts or truth. Truth is a person! His name is Jesus. Facts can be measured. For instance, you might feel tall, but the fact is different. You might feel fat, but the scale says you lost weight. You might feel responsible for your prodigal, but the fact is your child has free will, and they are responsible for their choices. It's important you accept this truth!

"

YOU MIGHT FEEL RESPONSIBLE FOR YOUR PRODIGAL, BUT THE FACT IS YOUR CHILD HAS FREE WILL, AND THEY ARE RESPONSIBLE FOR THEIR CHOICES.

When He gave free will, God accepted that He was not responsible for His children's actions. As parents, a good position to be in is when you not only understand free will but accept it.

As you walk through your prodigal parent process, you will have several moments of accepting your child's responsibility for how they use their free will. For example, remember when your child was given or earned their first car? You hoped they were responsible for following the rules like speed limits and turning signals. You hoped they would drive the car to school, church, or friends' house (you know, safe places). You hoped they wouldn't drive to parties with alcohol, drug houses, places for sexual opportunities, but every time they would drive off, only they were responsible for where they drove that car. This is illustrative of being a parent.

You may have carried them in the womb, and you gave them your best, but free will is a funny thing. They get to choose with their free will where they drive the car and who they let in the car with them.

"

WHEN YOU UNDERSTAND FREE WILL, YOU CAN LET OTHERS BE RESPONSIBLE FOR THEIR ATTITUDES, BELIEFS, BEHAVIORS, AND CHOICES IN ALL AREAS OF THEIR LIVES.

My point in this chapter is simple. You are part of a big experiment called free will. When you understand free will, you can let others be responsible for their attitudes, beliefs, behaviors, and choices in _all_ areas of their lives.

> **AT ANY POINT IN LIFE, A CHILD CAN CHOOSE TO CHANGE THEIR ENTIRE DIRECTION AND OUTCOME FOR THE LIFE GOD HAS GIVEN THEM.**

For me, if a child is a saint, they choose that path. If a child is a prodigal, they choose that path. At any point in life, a child can choose to change their entire direction and outcome for the life God has given them.

CHAPTER
Ten

OBJECT SYSTEM VS. RELATIONAL THINKING

This is our last chapter in understanding the prodigal process, and I am excited to move into the prodigal parent process. I do believe we have laid a good foundation for you to understand clearly, and in a multifaceted manner, your prodigal and the process they go through. Before we leave the land of the prodigal, there is one more topic that is helpful for parents of prodigals.

Earlier, when we discussed Romans chapter 1, where it talks about the prodigal's thinking becoming futile and hearts becoming darkened, we concluded this is a natural process that occurs. When our souls suppress the truth, we have to reorganize the way we process life. We change inside in a profound and significant manner; however, most often, both the prodigal and the parents have no language for what has occurred. As a parent, what you experience is they no longer respect you or care about your opinion. You experience that you no longer matter, but you are confused as to why. You observe these bizarre behaviors and beliefs from your prodigal that make no sense and are self-destructive, and you don't know why they can't see the consequences for these behaviors. Often you are dumbfounded and at a total loss as to what has happened to your child.

"

WHEN OUR SOULS SUPPRESS THE TRUTH, WE HAVE TO REORGANIZE THE WAY WE PROCESS LIFE.

When a soul suppresses a truth, they have to change how they view the world to be able to—in their mind—circumvent truth and do as they wish. In other words, this suppression creates an internal process that makes it morally acceptable to do something they know is unacceptable.

Nearly every week, I have the opportunity to explain this idea of the need to change one's thinking to beautiful, good-hearted, godly women who are confronted with infidelity. Many of the stories are the same. She married a man who loves her and Jesus, and they built a life together for years or decades, then one day, she discovers he has been looking at pornography or having an affair. She cannot comprehend how he could do such a crazy, selfish, bizarre thing to himself, her, and their children.

I have to explain to her that her husband had to suppress the truth in his heart to participate in the behavior he knows is unacceptable to God and her. In this process, he had not only to betray others, he had to betray himself. His self-betrayal and rejection of God put him into a place where he had to change how he processed life itself. Now, it is common that at this point in our discussion, she does not yet understand, so I continue on and explain the difference between object thinking and relational thinking.

OBJECT SYSTEM VS. RELATIONAL THINKING

Just as this husband went from one way of thinking to the opposite way, so did your prodigal. You taught your prodigal about right from wrong and how to live and treat others. They, too, had to switch the way they process life to make what they know to be unacceptable to God acceptable to themselves.

I want to educate you on two different and opposing operating systems humans can choose from. These systems are far apart as a Mac operating system is from a DOS operating system.

The first system is what I call Relational Reality. In this system, which is most likely the one you utilize to process life, you process everything around you from a relational perspective. In relational reality processing, there are three core beliefs you hold as true: people have value, there are rules, and there are consequences. I will explain each one briefly. Then I will do the same for the Object Operating System (the system for those who suppress the truth).

RELATIONAL REALITY
People have value

You believe you are in a relationship with God, and all His children have value. You view a soul, regardless of what it has done to itself or others, as having innate value. This core belief provides people the

respect they deserve because they are human beings. You do not want to hurt others; creating pain
for them intentionally would create internal pain
for yourself.

There are rules

As a soul that lives in relational reality, you accept
a moral universe. You acknowledge there is a God
in heaven and on earth, and you are not Him. You
accept it is immoral to lie, steal, cheat, or harm
others. You don't have to memorize these ideals—
they are a part of the very fabric of who you are.

There are consequences

We intuitively understand if we do something
wrong, there will be a consequence. We fear God,
and we know He rewards those who do right and
disciplines those that do otherwise (Hebrews 11:6).
This core belief allows you to plan ahead and not
take the wrong roads in life, saying no to the obvious and even less apparent temptations. You value
staying in the place of serving and being a good
soul to others.

As a believer and often a more "mature" adult, you
approach the world with a focus on reality that val-

ues relationships—people. You can't conceptualize loving in any other way; however, there is another process, and it results when we suppress the truth. This process is exactly the opposite of the relational reality—it won't make sense to you. Initially, you may not understand what I am about to share any more than the godly wife who was cheated on understands the behavior of her husband. However, if you, as a parent, can accept that this is most likely how your prodigal is processing life and relationships, it will not only make sense, but you will begin to take their actions less personally.

OBJECT OPERATING SYSTEM
People (souls) have no value

When a person rejects God and a relationship with Him, they diminish the value of all relationships. The result? People are no longer valued; they are merely objects to be used. Thus, if you have no value to the prodigal, they can choose to disregard, mistreat poorly, or even abuse you without remorse.

You see, value is assigned to an object based upon how much it can do for the prodigal. This is why your prodigal can ascribe value to people who may not necessarily be good; this other person supports their sin and enables them to believe they live in a world with no god. Since you don't support your prodigal's current and foreign worldview, you have little to no value to them. This change in processing is why you are discounted, disrespected, and not heard, because now you are not a soul that deserves respect but are just a thing to them (*until they repent*).

There are no rules

When you reject God, you no longer live in a moral universe where you are ultimately accountable for your beliefs and behaviors. There are no rules from God to follow, except the ones you make up for yourself. This is why your prodigal can steal from you, lie to you, blame you, manipulate you, and call you crazy if you get upset about it. When there are no rules, and people have no value, they become "king/queen of their world" and can do as they please with their objects called people. The objects should just go along with whatever they desire.

There are no consequences

In object reality, there are no consequences. This is why your prodigal can do or say anything, regardless of how wrong or hateful it might be, and are surprised if you have a reaction that is not supportive. This is why they may not pay a ticket, make payments on a credit card, pay their rent, or pay back the money they "borrowed.

Remember, it was the consequences of the wayward living of the son in the story in Luke 15 that causes him to repent and go home. The prodigal spent all his money, ended up having to get a job with the pigs, went hungry, and then woke up.

The object processing of life is about getting your way, and this is why yelling, disrespecting, and manipulating you can be acceptable to your prodigal.

Galatians 5:19-24 highlights this Object Operating System versus the Relational Reality. The first portion of the passage reveals the characteristics of the object way of processing life: "The acts of the flesh are obvious: sexual immorality, impurity, and debauchery; idolatry and witchcraft; hatred, discord, jealousy, fits of rage, selfish ambition, dissensions, factions, and envy; drunkenness, orgies, and the like. I warn you, as I did before, that those who live like this will not inherit the kingdom of God" (19-21). You can clearly see that in every sense, the person objectifies and takes advantage of others. This soul doesn't value others, and these behaviors manifest in a soul that wants to live for itself.

Now, contrast the object way to the relational processing found in verses 22 – 24. This person values others and lives accountable: "But the fruit of the Spirit is love, joy, peace, forbearance, kindness, goodness, faithfulness, gentleness and self-control. Against such things there is no law. Those who belong to Christ Jesus have crucified the flesh with its passions and desires." This soul honors God and values His children.

After reading the verses above, one can quickly assess which processing a person is operating in by how they treat people.

It is critical that parents of prodigals understand that they have likely been relegated to object status by a soul that is struggling to justify its behavior. While in this object operating system, prodigals can think what they think and do what they do, all while ignoring your heart. This is why they can lie, take money, dishonor your time, and feel no remorse about it, or worse, blame you for why they did it.

If someone uses a relational mindset to interpret object processing, they will be left dumbfounded because the behavior of sin (and the rejecting of God) doesn't make sense in a relational reality. Truth is truth, and sin is sin. But as prodigals move away from the truth, they move into object reality.

HERE IS AN EXAMPLE:

1. A prodigal child steals $200 out of his mother's purse.

2. The prodigal presumes his mother has no value; the mother can't believe it: "He loves me;" "He wouldn't do this to his mother." She is dumbfounded.

3. Now, if she can look through the lens of the object process and presume he believes she has no value, she will say, "I have no value to him. He believes there are no rules, so stealing is acceptable. He doesn't think we should talk about it because I left it out there to be stolen."

When considered through the lens of the Object Operating System, the behavior makes sense, even though in a relational reality, it is clearly wrong or unloving. But at the same time, unfortunately, this object reality way of thinking, especially if there is a sex, porn, alcohol, drug, or other addiction involved, is the way prodigals will approach life and relationships until they return whole-heartedly to God.

CHAPTER
Eleven
PARENT PROCESS

I hope you have gained both biblical and practical insight into the prodigal process in all the previous chapters. I hope it's made a significant difference in your heart, that independent of you or your spouse, your prodigal has taken a known journey away from God. I say known because millions of Christian parents have had one or more of their children walk this prodigal road for years or even decades. I hope, by now, you understand that you are not responsible for your prodigal's choices.

You may know of others that were not very good parents. You might know a couple who struggled with addiction, abuse (either giving it or receiving it), neglect, and immaturity, and yet their children follow God wholeheartedly. I am my example. My parents were not spiritual. I never saw a Bible and don't remember having one conversation about God. I grew up outside of the church, and then at age nineteen, I got saved. I decided to allow Christ to mature me from that point on.

"

THERE ARE FEW THINGS IN LIFE MORE CHALLENGING THAN WATCHING YOUR CHILD SELF-DESTRUCT.

Still holding onto the process that prodigals go through, I want to turn our attention to the prodigal parent processes. Parents of prodigals of every culture, age, and race suffer similar processes as their prodigal chooses to be a prodigal. There are few things in life more challenging than watching your child self-destruct. There are long sleepless nights as you feel hurt, angry, and sad at your child being so lost, confused, and in pain. There are difficult conversations, sometimes intense, between parents searching for the best way to respond to the prodigal's behavior or latest demand. Then there is also how this all affects siblings. And often, birthday celebrations are soured and vacations ruined because of the prodigal's erratic behavior or absence.

Sadly, unlike other events such as broken bones or poor grades, the prodigal experience isn't an event that lasts a short amount of time. The lives of prodigals are often measured in years of broken relationships. A prodigal's process starts well before we identify it, and the saga of a prodigal can go on for years, decades, spanning sometimes several stages of life. This ongoing, prolonged bruising can easily be the heaviest burden you will bear as a parent. Often, you don't want to talk about your prodigal. You do your best to be polite or change the subject when someone asks how your prodigal is doing. You might even pull away from couples you know so you can avoid conversations about your prodigal. Even with God, you can feel unheard, frustrated that your prodigal isn't changing.

A PRODIGAL'S PROCESS STARTS WELL BEFORE WE IDENTIFY IT.

And even at church, your "place of hope," you never hear a sermon on the parent of a prodigal even though a significant number of families are suffering from the pain of having a prodigal, so you feel yor pain is unheard or unimportant. As I reflect on my nearly forty years of going to church every week, I don't recall one sermon or comment on the pain as a parent of a prodigal.

Many churches don't know what to do when it comes to parents of prodigals. They will pray for you in a well-meaning manner; however, to help you feel and process your pain, and help you make the tough decisions, they have no class for that (until now, I hope). Even the larger churches with programs for men's issues, grief classes, and divorce care are often silent on parents of prodigals. It's not that they don't care; they often have no tools in their toolbox to offer you.

> **I WANT YOU TO KNOW THAT YOU ARE NOT ALONE IN THIS PROCESS OF BEING A PRODIGAL'S PARENT.**

That is where the rest of these pages will come in: to fill in the gap for yourself and to help you start a parent prodigal support group if you choose. I want you to know that you are not alone in this process of being a prodigal's parent and to sense the closeness that comes from knowing that faithful moms and dads are struggling with the very same pain and confusion. Most importantly, God knows, He cares, and He, through the Holy Spirit, is intimately involved.

I also want to offer you language to be able to communicate better what you are experiencing. When you assign clarifying language to what you are experiencing, I firmly believe it makes the process much more understandable and manageable.

Also, in future chapters, I will invite you to participate in a variety of exercises. These exercises have proven fruitful with my clients for decades. If you encounter an exercise that is challenging or is outside of your comfort zone, I ask that you embrace it, complete it, and then have an opinion about it. I understand it is easy to skip over sections like these, but when people reach a point of crisis and commit to a counseling intensive, and we complete these exercises, it is life-changing for them.

Thus, you can complete some significant emotional and spiritual healing by thoroughly engaging with the following chapters. Also, I have created the *Prodigal Parent Process* DVD and workbook to facilitate your thinking further and help you make progress on your prodigal parent process. Through these resources, I will walk you through processes to help you heal as you continue to navigate the various aspects of what you have experienced because of your prodigal.

As you go through the next pages, most of the work will have to do with healing your heart from what has happened or is currently happening with your prodigal. But, you will also be introduced to what you can do to heal aspects of your prodigal impact on your relationship with your spouse. And, you will also be given ideas to help you navigate some of the impacts the prodigal has had on other children in your family.

Lastly, there are ideas to help you cross some bridges with your prodigals if you feel it's appropriate.

Writing what we will cover in the next few chapters gives you the idea that the healing part of the prodigal parent process will be quite the undertaking. So let me say up front, I am very proud of you for walking through this and seeking to heal an area that needs to be healed so you can be an awesome follower of the Lord Jesus Christ and an incredible spouse and parent.

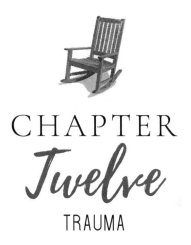

CHAPTER
Twelve
TRAUMA

Day in and day out, for more than thirty years, I have been working with men and women who have experienced trauma; I am the founder of the Partner Betrayal Trauma movement, which is for women who have experienced infidelity, sex addition, or intimacy anorexia from their husbands. Most of my thousands of clients have experienced sexual, physical, or emotional trauma that they have had to work through to heal.

Generally, trauma results from being abused, neglected, or experiencing something outside the normal range of experience. This trauma would be similar to that of fighting a war, having your life threatened, being rape, or even just watching any of this occur.

In the case of the prodigal parent process, trauma can result from having a prodigal child. What do I mean? It can be like watching your child play Russian roulette with their lives even though you have dreams for them individually and as part of the family unit. As they make poor relationship choices, abuse alcohol, drugs, and sex in unhealthy ways, destroy opportunities, get fired, have accidents, or any other kind of drama or chaos, their individual and collective experiences are traumatic for you.

THE IMPACTS OF A PRODIGAL ON A PARENT ARE VERY REAL.

This trauma is a whole person trauma; it affects all of who you are as a parent—spirit, soul, and body. Your spouse is also experiencing this trauma. Each parent will respond differently, but it's important to remember, they are experiencing trauma as well. The impacts of a prodigal on a parent are very real. The most common are a sense of antipathy, distraction, being less focused, depression, Post Traumatic Stress Disorder, grieving spells, unexplained crying, bad dreams, and the list goes on and on.

I will walk you through the various impacts you may experience and share ideas to help you get through this trauma. But know, trauma affects everyone and every couple differently; this is no different when it comes to having a prodigal child. Your gender, age, emotional maturity, possible history with addictions, your own trauma, sexual abuse, and general personality are all variables in the way you might handle the trauma of having a prodigal child.

In these pages, I want to walk through some of the major ways I have seen mothers and fathers impacted by the trauma of having a prodigal son or daughter.

Depression

With all the energy you expend from being concerned, overwhelmed, hopeless, and powerless over your child's behavior, it can drain you. You are the one who sits on the sofa staring out the window, wondering what the prodigal is doing and when this will all stop. You're crying out to God. You wake up early in the morning, unable to sleep because you learned something negative about your prodigal's life. If this energy drain goes on for a while, and it usually does, you can exhibit signs of clinical depression.

Let's quickly go through the symptoms of depression:

- Feelings of worthlessness
- Difficulty concentrating
- Difficulty making decisions
- Weight gain/loss
- Suicidal thoughts
- Low energy
- Sleep disturbance
- Feelings of hopelessness
- Angry outbursts
- Loss of interest in pleasure, including sex

Depression is real. It can happen to the most faith-filled person, and it would be a very normal reaction to having a prodigal child. So, if you are having even a few of the symptoms listed above, you will want to address this as early as possible. As I often tell my clients, talk to your doctor about this and be sure you get cortisol levels, hormones, and thyroid checked. Why? Because depression symptoms can be mimicked if one has low testosterone and thyroid—this is true for both men and women.

Medicating

If throughout your life, you have a pattern of medicating difficult feelings, you can be prone to use more during this time. What do I mean by medicating? Excessive consumption of alcohol or overeating, overworking and busyness, spending hours each day watching television or on social media, viewing pornography, and a reliance on prescription drugs are just a few examples. If you are medicating your pain in these or other ways, you could be creating an addiction yourself.

How do you know if you are medicating through a substance or behaviors? The following can help you determine if you are.

- Tried to stop
- Promises to stop
- Consequences
- Using after consequences
- Use or do more
- Takes more to have an impact

- Takes more time
- Withdrawals if you can't have or do
- Decrease in other activities

If you have three or more of the above symptoms, you could be using a substance or activity to medicate.

I realize I mentioned this earlier; however, it is very important that you are honest with yourself. If you are actively in an addiction, *you are actively destroying yourself, your marriage, and your family.* Your pain is the problem! It is important that you do not medicate it; rather, you must feel it, talk about it, and grieve it. Remember, Christ, who lives *in you*, was beaten beyond recognition, placed on a cross, and refused to take narcotics offered to Him to dull the pain. Although you have a prodigal for a season, maybe even a long season, you will want to actively resist medicating your soul and life as a means to solve your pain.

Post-Traumatic Stress Disorder (PTSD)

Classic PTSD has to do with watching or experiencing something horrific, attempted murder, rape, etc., personally. When you are in a primary relationship (husband/wife or parent/child), you can experience PTSD symptoms from this person's real pain or fear. And this is especially true if they persist in thinking and behavior that is self-destructive. Some of the symptoms of PTSD are:

- Having memories/flashbacks/nightmares or terrors
- For instance, them yelling at you, a car accident, calls from jail, their spouse calling you, etc.
- Being triggered or distressed when witnessing similar events in others' lives or even media
- Your child gets arrested for burglary, and when you see this story in a film, you are triggered
- Avoiding plans, people, or events that pertain to behaviors of your prodigal
- Ongoing negative thinking about yourself or others in general
- Hopelessness
- Pulling away from other relationships
- DistractionNot enjoying activities
- Have challenges feeling up/happy or positive
- Memory issues
- Nervous feeling

- Sleep issues/disturbances
- Overwhelming guilt/shame
- Problems with typically normal bodily functions, such as using the restroom

These symptoms can come and go, and some run parallel to depression. Parents having PTSD are often unaware that this is what they are experiencing, and because they don't know the common symptoms, they can't assess their own behavior and understand this is a normal response to having a prodigal. Also, for some parents of prodigals, knowing what is happening to them can lessen the effect their prodigal has on their self-esteem. Instead of believing the lie that there is something wrong with you, you can accept that there is something wrong that is affecting you.

If you are experiencing several of the PTSD symptoms listed above, it's probably good to talk to a therapist, or if your church has a group for parents of prodigals, then checking in with a same gender person could be helpful.

Remember, this prodigal process is *not about you*, even though it impacts you. I find the more a parent tries to take responsibility and blame themselves or their spouse for what has happened, the more severe PTSD symptoms can be experienced. Like I just mentioned, being a prodigal is, without exception, your child's choice; you can be free from blame or false guilt. Not falsely blaming yourself or your spouse can give you more energy in your life. And this is good because you will be healthier when your prodigal returns to God and you.

CHAPTER
Thirteen
GRIEF

As a parent of a prodigal, you may have encountered many losses. As you move through the months, years, or decades that your child chooses to be a prodigal, you will grieve more than once. When you can self-identify that you are grieving and identify the stage of grief you're in, it won't take the pain of that stage away, but it will allow you to see where you are in the process and help you to grieve.

Grieving is normal and helpful, but how grief will manifest in you is different than how it will manifest in someone else, including your spouse if you are married. And even if you are both Christians, you will rarely be in the same stage of grief at the same time, be grieving on the same issue, or experience your losses from your prodigal's choices in the same way.

Here are a few of the losses you may experience from your prodigal:

- Loss of who you thought they were
- Loss of your dreams for them
- Loss of a "Christian" family
- Loss of seeing grandchildren
- Loss of reputation
- Loss of peace in your family
- Loss of energy, time, resourcesThe loss of family events, holidays, birthdays, and so much more

In the 1960s, Kubler-Ross gave us the Grief Process. I want to apply that process for the parents of prodigals.

Grief is a known process we go through when a tragedy occurs, and in this case, every parent of a prodigal has had a moment, a wake-up call, when they were forced to face that their son or daughter is not who they thought they were. Some "wake-up" examples could be:

- A call from the police
- Telling you they are pregnant or got someone pregnant
- Finding drugs
- Suicide attempt
- Drunk driving

When this "bad reality" or "wake-up call" takes place, you begin the grieving process.

The grieving process happens so we can process the tragedy in manageable pieces because it's so big we can't process or accept it all at once. There are six steps to the Grief Process. You may have gone through some of these stages already; however, depending on the latest event with your prodigal, you may cycle through grief repeatedly.

Stage 1: Shock

This can be overwhelming, like a numb feeling. In shock, you are faced with the darker side of your child that resembles Romans 1:22 "...their foolish hearts were darkened." On this darker side, you could be exposed to their connection with porn, drugs, or sex. Of course, this is the opposite of what you were thinking and believing about your child.

And the realization usually comes so quickly; it is such a surprise, the initial shock can last for days. Eventually, this stage will end, and you will start moving forward to other stages. One caveat is, as your prodigal goes further down the road, their behaviors can get worse, or your discovery of even more darkness can return you to the shock state of the grief process.

Stage 2: Denial

Denial can last hours to decades. No good Christian parent wants to admit their child has sinned, hardened their heart, rejected God, and that they are indifferent toward you and your faith and values. Many parents simply deny it, making excuses or explaining it away saying,

- This is just a stage they are going through.
- They are just finding themselves.
- This is "so-and-so's" fault.
- They really didn't do "_____" act.
- They really didn't mean to do "_____" act.
- They won't do "_____" act again.

These are just a few. There are hundreds of other things we as parents can tell ourselves in order not to accept that our child is a prodigal, when in reality, the prodigal has rejected God as an authority in their life. They've created their own world, and sin is in that world. I admit, this is very hard to accept about your child, so this is why denial has such a grip on parents.

> **"**
> THE TRUTH IS YOU DIDN'T FAIL BECAUSE BEING A PRODIGAL IS NOT A PARENTING ISSUE; IT'S A FREE WILL AND RELATIONSHIP WITH GOD ISSUE.

Denial is about protecting you from accepting the truth about your child. Sometimes, in a misguided way, especially if you are blaming yourself or your spouse, this denial stage may protect you from believing you failed. The truth is _you didn't fail_ because being a prodigal is not a parenting issue; it's a free will and relationship with God issue. Don't choose to believe the lie that the reason your child is a prodigal is because of a parenting issue; the reality is, it's not.

Stage 3: Anger

Now we are getting somewhere. You are starting to feel some feelings. It is normal to feel outraged after all you have done—all the sacrifices you have made. You may even angrily tell your prodigal, "We didn't raise you this way!" You believe this because this was not supposed to be the outcome of all your effort and love. Your anger is legitimate. Even God got angry at Israel when they became prodigals again and again. Anger means you are starting to process the pain of having a prodigal in your life.

> ANGER MEANS YOU ARE STARTING TO PROCESS THE PAIN OF HAVING A PRODIGAL IN YOUR LIFE.

In the next chapter, I'm going to give you a tool called *cleansing the temple* to help you and your body heal from your prodigal's choice to reject God.

Stage 4: Bargaining

Bargaining is a tricky stage of grief. It's where you're trying to process the pain while you are also trying to figure out where to place the blame. Bargaining can go something like this:

- If "X" did or didn't happen, then my child would not be a prodigal.
- If I would have spent more time with them,

then my child would not be a prodigal.

- If my spouse would or wouldn't have done "X," then my child would not be a prodigal.
- If they didn't date that person, then my child would not be a prodigal.
- If they didn't find porn on the internet, then my child would not be a prodigal.

Basically, if you are "if-ing," you are bargaining.

The truth is your prodigal, in their heart, rejected God and started ruling their life as their only authority. This is the _only_ reason they are a prodigal. Their choice to be a prodigal is not about you, your spouse, or anyone or any circumstances. This is the path they have chosen. The decision to reject God is exclusively theirs.

> **THEIR CHOICE TO BE A PRODIGAL IS NOT ABOUT YOU, YOUR SPOUSE, OR ANYONE OR ANY CIRCUMSTANCES.**

Stage 5: Sadness

Now that your heart is feeling the pain and loss of your prodigal, you are accepting their rejection of God, you, your family values, and that you have no value to them. You are sad, and this can last days, weeks, or months. I acknowledge how sad it is when they chose to be a prodigal. It's sad you won't have the complete Christian family you hoped for, and in many cases, legitimately deserve if parenting was cause and effect, but it's not (more on this later). Allow yourself to be sad, cry, pray, journal, talk to a friend or someone else who is a parent of a prodigal.

"

ALLOW YOURSELF TO BE SAD, CRY, PRAY, JOURNAL, TALK TO A FRIEND OR SOMEONE ELSE WHO IS A PARENT OF A PRODIGAL.

Stage 6: Acceptance

Acceptance is the final stage of grief. In this stage, you accept their condition as it is. It can take months, years, or even decades for some parents to be able to remain in a state of acceptance that their child has chosen and continues to choose the path of a prodigal. What does acceptance sound like?

- My child is in rebellion against God.
- My child is playing by their own rules.
- My child does not value our values or us.
- My child has done this to themselves.

- My child can't understand my pain or the pain they have created in our family.
- My child is a prodigal, and until that changes, not much can be expected from them.
- My child being a prodigal is not my or my spouses' fault.

All of these statements are true. When you can accept this, you are in acceptance. Acceptance gets rid of false guilt, blame, or any false shame you may carry. Acceptance keeps you free from thinking you are going to make the difference. Acceptance allows you to trust God without trying to manipulate the child or their circumstances.

> **"**
> ACCEPTANCE ALLOWS YOU TO TRUST GOD WITHOUT TRYING TO MANIPULATE THE CHILD OR THEIR CIRCUMSTANCES.

Yes, grief will come and go; you can't avoid it, and neither can your spouse, but understanding it can help you to be compassionate toward yourself and your spouse. Grief can give you a language to both identify and express your feelings and permission to be where you are, be it denial, anger, bargaining, or sadness.

I recommend having a godly friend of the same gender you can rely upon to process your grief. This can help you and your marriage by making it so you do not have to carry the entire weight of the grief by yourself.

"

GRIEF CAN GIVE YOU A LANGUAGE TO BOTH IDENTIFY AND EXPRESS YOUR FEELINGS AND PERMISSION TO BE WHERE YOU ARE.

You and your spouse will grieve. This chapter might be one you revisit to help you as you go through another cycle of grief. Grief is good because it allows you to accept the painful reality that you are a parent of a prodigal. And by all means, invite Christ into each stage of the grieving cycle for your prodigal.

CHAPTER

Fourteen

ANGER

Anger is definitely something we need to investigate as a parent of a prodigal. You and your spouse are going to experience and express anger differently and at different times throughout your prodigal's ongoing choices.

I find this topic of anger a challenge for some parents of prodigals. Some have a real challenge processing, feeling, or expressing their anger about their prodigal's choices. Some have a real challenge admitting that they are angry, actually enraged at their prodigal. Admitting will be the first step toward owning and releasing your anger.

ADMITTING WILL BE THE FIRST STEP TOWARD OWNING AND RELEASING YOUR ANGER.

Imagine for a moment any other person who lied to you, lied about you, broke your spouse's heart, hurt all your other children, or was unreliable or unpredictable; you would have legitimate anger toward them. Of course, you would be angry if you were treated like an object that has no value, manipulated, and let down repeatedly. This behavior is what many parents of prodigals experience over time from their prodigal child.

Anger is legitimate. God expressed anger with Israel on more than one occasion as they rejected Him and chose to live as a prodigal from Him. God got so mad at mankind, "[He] regretted that he had made human beings on the earth, and his heart was deeply troubled" (Genesis 6:6). It is legitimate and acceptable to be angry at your prodigal's behavior. The Scripture says, "Be angry and sin not" (Ephesians 4:26). What's interesting to me is this verse says, "Be angry." In other passages of scripture, we are commanded to be kind, loving, generous, etc. Here we are instructed to express our anger but to do so without sin. Thus, I believe it is acceptable to be angry. A prodigal can do or say several things that can provoke real anger.

I want to show you an exercise I use with sexual addicts, rape victims, spouses of betrayal, whether from sex addiction or intimacy anorexia. This exercise has helped thousands release anger and move toward freedom from the consequences of holding this legitimate rage inside their body and soul. We call this exercise *cleansing the temple*, taken from Jesus cleansing the temple recorded in all four gospels:

> Jesus entered the temple and drove out all who were buying and selling there. He overturned the tables of the money-changers and the benches of those selling doves.

Matthew 21:12

> On reaching Jerusalem, Jesus entered the temple area and began driving out those who were buying and selling there. He overturned the tables of the money-changers and the benches of those selling doves.

Mark 11:15

Then he entered the temple area and began driving out those who were selling.

Luke 19:45

In the temple courts he found men selling cattle, sheep and doves, and others sitting at tables exchanging money. So he made a whip out of cords, and drove all from the temple area, both sheep and cattle; he scattered the coins of the money changers and overturned their tables. To those who sold doves he said, "Get these out of here! How dare you turn my Father's house into a market!"

John 2:14-16

Rarely is something in all four gospels. This was not only a significant event, it was also a process in which Jesus was showing us how to clean our temples when others choose to defile or mistreat us. In each gospel account, Jesus,

- Identified the sin
- Engaged his anger physically
- The temple was cleansed

You know you are that temple. 1 Corinthians 3:16 reads, "Don't you know that you yourselves are God's temple." Your prodigal's choices have defiled your life and caused you all kinds of pain. And only you, by the grace of God, can clean your temple.

This is an important point that only you can clean your own temple. The reason Jesus—and no one else—could clean the temple is because it was His temple. I would love to have the ability to clean other people's temples from trauma, but I can't: only they can.

> **ONLY YOU, BY THE GRACE OF GOD, CAN CLEAN YOUR TEMPLE.**

When my clients say, "Dr. Weiss, I can't do that." I kindly remind them of the scripture Philippians 4:13, "I can do everything through Him who gives me strength." They smile, and then we proceed. Afterward, they are so relieved and grateful that they cleansed their temple.

Earlier I wrote I would share some exercises with you, but you only benefit from doing them. As I explain this, prepare to do this work and only have an opinion after you do this exercise.

Here is the process:

1. Write an anger letter to the prodigal, one they will never see. Get to a private place and physically write out your hurt and anger toward your prodigal. Write it, don't type it. Write it as if you could put them in a padded room for ten minutes and go off. Don't Christianize it, say I forgive you (that's in a later chapter), or attend to your language or grammar. No other person will see this letter. When you finish all the steps of *cleansing the temple*, destroy this letter.

2. By yourself, read it out loud. Read every word of your letter out loud.

3. Find something safe to hit with and something safe to hit. I suggest plastic You are preparing to engage your anger physically, just as Jesus did.

4. Warm up. Take your bat and hit the bed a few times with a high level of intensity (small, medium, or large). You can also warm up using the

word "no" as a vocal warm-up. In the next step, you will not be using the word no.

5. Go ballistic. Here, I want you just to let it all out. You can say what you need to. Hit while you're voicing your anger. This should look like losing control. You are experiencing a three-dimensional trauma. This can take anywhere from 5 to 20 minutes. Give yourself total privacy while doing this exercise. If you have any medical concerns, talk to your doctor before doing this.

This is very important for your body to pull this rage out of your body. Holding this rage can have so many bad effects on you. You may need to repeat this periodically as the prodigal is prone to re-injure you repeatedly.

In every gospel account, Jesus cleansed the temple before he said, "Father forgive them." We will talk about forgiveness next.

For now, set a day and time you will do this. Be accountable to your friend, support person, or your spouse to get this accomplished. This will be hard, but it feels so much better after you do it.

CHAPTER
Fifteen
FORGIVENESS

Forgiveness is a very important part of the prodigal parent process. The prodigal will be a prodigal as long as they choose to be. They will make mistakes and poor choices, have poor relationships, and bring ongoing disappointments, hurts to your heart and to the hearts of your spouse and family.

The prodigal is living in a self-created, self-centered world, thrashing around in life avoiding the authority of Christ. Their soul, as we have learned, is in pain from not being led by the Holy Spirit. This will bring guaranteed pain to oneself and to all who genuinely love them.

In the last chapter, I discussed anger and the cleaning the temple exercise. That exercise is a precursor to being able to arrive at and remain in a state of forgiveness. In every gospel account, the act of cleansing the temple preceded "Father, forgive them," as Jesus hung on a cross, paying the penalty for our sins.

66

FORGIVENESS IS A VERY IMPORTANT PART OF THE PARENT PRODIGAL PROCESS.

I have worked with thousands of clients who have been sexually abused, betrayed, or neglected by their spouse or family. When they attend a 5-Day Counseling Intensive with me, one of the first things I have them do is to complete the *cleansing the temple* exercise. Then, in the intensive, they complete their forgiveness work. Much to their surprise, they are able to forgive. I will explain this forgiveness work and introduce you to a *forgiveness exercise* later in this chapter. I strongly recommend you and your spouse complete after you have already done the *cleansing the temple* exercise.

I want to share with you a few myths about forgiveness; I initially wrote this in my book *The 7*

Love Agreements, published by Charisma House. I find confronting these myths can be helpful when we are faced with the talk of forgiveness. Here are three myths to know about forgiveness before you move to forgive your prodigal or others.

<u>*Myth #1*</u>: *I have to confront them to offer them my forgiveness.*

People have ideas about forgiveness that can hinder them from being able to forgive a person. The first myth I often encounter with a client is the idea that somehow the person has to be present for me to forgive them. They believe that the person must be confronted about how they abused, neglected, and lied, and if the person says "forgive me," then the exchange could actually happen. Now, if the offending person isn't mature enough to own their own sin toward you, they might not be mature enough to ask for forgiveness when confronted. As we have discussed, prodigals are generally not in a mature state while choosing to become and remain a prodigal.

The forgiveness you will be giving to your prodigal over the months, years, or multiple years will be a choice. Forgiveness is entirely your choice. The other person does not need to be present for the transaction of forgiveness to occur.

Myth #2: The person is going to have to repent first

Thank God the person does not have to repent before we can forgive them. If this were true, we would have to wait so long for so many to repent before we are able to forgive them.

Christ gave us the power to forgive at our will. We never need anyone to repent for us to forgive. Scripture commands us to forgive. It puts the onus on us to take the initiative to forgive instead of having to wait for an immature person even to realize they need to be forgiven. Now, if we had to wait, every believer would be unable to forgive another until the person repented. But, Christ died for us and forgave all of humanity at the cross well before billions of us were even born.

"

CHRIST GAVE US THE POWER TO FORGIVE AT OUR WILL.

You do not need your prodigal son or daughter to repent for you to forgive them. Forgiving, in general, keeps your heart soft. I tell couples who are attending pre-marriage conferences, you can decide the day you get married to forgive every sin of your spouse (because you are marrying a sinner), or you can wait, judge, and decide on every sin as you journey through the marriage. The power to decide to forgive is always ours.

Myth #3 I have to see change for me to forgive

Others, thankfully, do not have to change one bit for me to forgive. If you or I have to wait for change to occur to release the gift of forgiveness, we could be stuck. Fortunately, they don't have to repent or change for me to forgive them. This truth allows me to forgive anyone at any time. I am in the driver's seat of forgiveness in my life. This allows me to obey the command to forgive without any hindrance in any form.

As a psychologist, I would add that forgiveness is different from trust. Even if you forgive your prodigal (or anyone else), you might still double-check the facts before believing them in the future. You might want a drug test or polygraph before believing that they have quit. You might want to observe them become faithful with little before giving them more. You can forgive and still have boundaries. It is good to verify before trusting the prodigal.

"

FORGIVENESS IS DIFFERENT FROM TRUST.

A FORGIVENESS EXERCISE

I want to give you a *forgiveness exercise* you can use with your prodigal or anyone in your life who needs forgiveness. I will say that doing the *cleansing the temple* exercise first will make this exercise much more effective. What I like about this exercise is you can complete it at any time. You also do not need the other person's permission or involvement in any way for this to be effective. You can repeat this exercise to keep forgiving. You can keep your heart clean no matter who sins against you from here on.

To do this exercise, you will want privacy; make sure you're alone, or the door is locked so you will not be disturbed. Also, place your cell phone in another room so you will not be distracted or interrupted.

You will need two chairs to complete this exercise.

We will identify these two chairs, facing each other, as chair one and chair two. Start the exercise sitting in chair one facing the empty chair two. In chair one, you will be conducting a role play. You are playing the role of your prodigal as if they had a clear, mature mind. As a mature version of your prodigal, you are apologizing to your parent and asking for forgiveness.

Let's suppose your prodigal's name is John, and he was apologizing to his mother. In chair one, you role-play John talking to his mother (assuming you are his mother): "Mom, I need you to forgive me for how much I embarrassed you by smoking at school. I need you to forgive me for _____." (Depending on your child's story, this could go on for ten to thirty minutes.) When "John" is done apologizing, switch to chare two and respond as yourself.

You can respond any way you wish, but it important you are honest. You might not be able to forgive your child just yet. You might only be able to forgive some of their actions. And you may be able to offer forgiveness for any and all pain caused by your prodigal. This exercise is not intended to force you to forgive. It's to help you discover where you are in the process of forgiving. I have heard every kind of response from "No way, I do not forgive you," to "I love you, I forgive you," to "I am forgiving you for myself so I can move on." Again, seek an honest response.

If you were able to say, "John, I forgive you," then physically stand up and go put yourself in John's chair, chair number one, and reply as John to the parent (in the empty chair). John might say, "Thank you so much, mom/dad." When John responds to the forgiveness, the exercise is complete. Let's review:

1. In chair one, you, as the prodigal, ask for forgiveness from you, who is supposedly sitting in the empty chair.

2. Switching to chair two, you respond to this request to be forgiven.

3. If you are able to forgive, go back to chair one and, as your prodigal, thank your parent.

4. If you are still in the process of forgiving, repeat the exercise at a later date.

If you discover you are in the process of forgiving,

I recommend you complete this exercise once a month or whenever the Holy Spirit prompts you.

Your prodigal journey is unique to you and your family. You will have experience a variety of pains with your prodigal. Sadly, this prodigal process can definitely be longer than any parent would wish for. You can utilize this *forgiveness exercise* throughout your journey. This exercise can give you a tool, so you know where your heart is in the process.

CHAPTER
Sixteen
CAUSE AND EFFECT

One of the most significant undermining ideas that can make the prodigal parent process more challenging is the idea of cause and effect. And this is understandable; even as an infant, we learn cause and effect: if we push this, it moves, or it makes noise. Today, cause and effect is engrained in our Christian walk. If we follow God, then His promises occur.

This idea of cause and effect is active in many areas of life. You can reflect on your life and quickly realize the cycles of cause and effect. You can see the seasons of discipline, training, education, or hard work which resulted in being compensated or rewarded. On the flip side, you can observe the bad choices and the resulting consequences as well.

We are rewarded and have consequences in life largely by cause and effect. If we save money, we have wealth. If we eat reasonably and exercise, we have health. We go to school, and we learn. If we work hard, we get raises or promoted.

When it comes to parenting, we, in our deepest heart, can easily believe, "If I am a good parent, I should have good children who become good adults." As Christians, we can even take this further, saying, "If I am a good Christian parent, I should have Christian children who love Jesus and grow up to Christian adults who have Christian children." And ideally, that "should" happen. However, free will exists in this equation, and the outcomes are unknown and unpredictable. In an earlier chapter, I discussed free will at length and what a unique gift it was to mankind. Free will abolishes any form of cause and effect when it comes to parenting.

Your prodigal, from birth, could independently testify of your parenting, love, and sacrifice and still, by choice, reject you, your values, and God.

You, like God, have gambled by giving birth to a creature with free will.

66

FREE WILL ABOLISHES ANY FORM OF CAUSE AND EFFECT WHEN IT COMES TO PARENTING.

Free will is the eliminator of cause and effect. Free will prevents known outcomes in parenting. The tighter you hold on to any notion of cause and effect as a parent, the more you will unnecessarily experience pain.

You are not the only good Christian couple who has a prodigal. As I have been sharing this idea of the prodigal parent process, almost 50 percent of parents tell me a story of one or more of their children who got involved with the wrong crowd and ventured into drugs, porn, sex, or new age ideology and have walked away from Christ, the church, and their family.

I want to break this idea of cause and effect. As a parent, your job is to create the environment, instruction, discipline, and to provide as best you can. That's it. You are not able to determine good outcomes as a result of your parenting. You are not responsible for the outcome. God doesn't hold you accountable for your child's free will choice to follow Him wholeheartedly or not. That is each individual's choice.

＂

GOD DOESN'T HOLD YOU ACCOUNTABLE FOR YOUR
CHILD'S FREE WILL CHOICE TO FOLLOW
HIM WHOLEHEARTEDLY OR NOT.

Free will eradicates the possibility of cause and effect. This doesn't stop at parenting. It includes employees, volunteers, church members, and leaders. People are free will agents until death. When you can relinquish cause and effect, blame dissolves. When you fully and truly relinquish any notion of cause and effect, you can progress through the bargaining stage of grief much more easily. When you acknowledge and accept there is nothing you could have done to guarantee your child would never become a prodigal, then you are free from the damage of misapplying cause and effect to your parenting and your prodigal's choices.

I have seen emotional chains fall off of mother and father when they can release cause and effect and fully embrace free will. When this occurs, they are able to live in reality.

When we agree that children have free will, we, like God, can:

- Create an environment
- Establish expectations
- Allow choices
- Allow consequences- good and bad

As parents, we don't want to talk about our prodigals until we feel safe that someone will be compassionate and not blame us for doing something wrong with us. We must first begin with God's perspective (after all, He was the first prodigal parent). And when we learn that God does not blame us for the decision our child makes to become a prodigal, then we can more fully embrace our role as parents without the undue pain of blaming ourselves or fearing blame from others.

If you keep "should-ing" on yourself, you will stay stuck, chasing a lie and suffering throughout it all.

CHAPTER
Seventeen
POWERLESS

In the recovery community, the word *powerless* is a big word. If you ever go to a twelve-step group, you will either hear the word as someone shares, or you will see it on the wall somewhere. This is a fundamental concept in addiction recovery of every type. I have written twelve-step workbooks on sex addiction, intimacy anorexia, general addiction, partners of sex addicts, and partner betrayal trauma. In each of these, I detail the concept of powerless.

Powerless means without power, just like jobless means without a job. A healthy parent of a prodigal admits and accepts they have no power to determine the outcome of their child's life. The challenge is that one could read this book, go through the DVD, and complete the *Prodigal Parent Process* workbook and still struggle with the idea they have 1%, 10%, 50%, etc., amount of power to control their child's future.

<blockquote>
A HEALTHY PARENT OF A PRODIGAL ADMITS AND ACCEPTS THEY HAVE NO POWER TO DETERMINE THE OUTCOME OF THEIR CHILD'S LIFE.
</blockquote>

I acknowledge that it is very difficult to admit that you are powerless. Admitting that you're powerless is enormous, and its implication is it brings freedom. And, this admission is an acknowledgment of reality, which is always a good thing. Now what such an admission does not mean is that you should cease hoping, believing, or praying that your child will return. Being powerless is not the same as being helpless. God is our strength and our help!

Since our children have free will, we don't have the power to compel them to choose to believe in or follow Christ. We can't even control their decisions to ensure they choose what is good, best, or even what just makes sense. Seriously, and I do mean seriously, no parent can make their child do anything. Every person, including our bundles of joy, is born with free will, and they have a mind, spirit, sexuality, and intellect that is all their own. This is a beautiful, wild experiment that God has designed and the we and our children are a part of.

Every parent wants this power; some are in denial that they have this power and believe if they act a certain way, then the child will change. As we learned earlier, this could also be the bargaining stage of grieving.

> "
> WHEN YOU GRASP AND BELIEVE YOU ARE POWERLESS OVER OTHERS—ESPECIALLY YOUR PRODIGAL— YOU ARE IN REALITY.

When you grasp and believe you are powerless over others—especially your prodigal—you are in reality. It begins with admitting and transitions into acceptance. What do you need to admit? That it is your prodigal's heart that believes what it believes, and only when they choose, by the grace of God and the work of the Holy Spirit, will their behavior change.

When we believe we are powerless, we act and re-act differently toward our prodigal. There is a shift in how we view their actions and thinking, recognizing it to be about them and not about us. When you turn the prodigal son or daughter over to God, trusting God and not your parental superpowers, you are in reality.

The great thing about being powerless is you are free of the outcome, free from manipulation, and free from the angst of bargaining. You are free from the treadmill of trying harder and much of the emotional ups and downs that go with running a race that you are never going to win.

"

WHEN YOU ACCEPT POWERLESSNESS OVER YOUR PRODIGAL, AND YOU GIVE THIS SAME POWERLESS GIFT TO YOUR SPOUSE.

When you accept powerlessness over your prodigal, and you give this same powerless gift to your spouse as you can see your spouse with much more compassion. You can stop demanding that your spouse has parental superpowers. You can stop blaming your spouse for not having fixed this prodigal. You can go embrace being lovers instead of two people overwhelmed by an unfixable problem. This allows you so much freedom in your marriage—believing and accepting you and your spouse are powerless.

Now, a quick assignment. I want you to express this truth out loud, whether you believe it or not. Say that you are powerless over your prodigal. Three times, say, "I am powerless over (name)."

How do you feel when you said that? Peaceful, queasy, didn't like it, frustrated? If you or your body are resistant to this idea, you might still be believing you are in control. This could be denial, bargaining, or even sadness preventing you from feeling anger at them—but it's not reality. When you can say out loud three times, "I am powerless over (name)," and your body stays at peace, you are likely accepting your true condition of powerless. I find when clients are more in reality, they make healthier decisions for themselves and others.

I would suggest you regularly confess, "Lord, I am powerless over my prodigal, and I turn them fully over to You. I trust You, not myself, to help them see how good You are." When I go to the Father, acknowledging my emptiness, my experience is I feel more of His amazingness. When I accept my pow-erlessness over anything, I'm acknowledging I am a sheep, and He alone is the Shepherd. I can follow Him and not need to know where I am going. My heart is glad when I am held in the hand of a God who, at His core, is LOVE.

CHAPTER
Eighteen
PROVERBS 22:6

No conversation of prodigals would be complete without Proverbs 22:6. This verse is a hope for many parents of prodigals. As a parent, you have probably prayed this scripture. You might have even reminded God of His Word. I feel it's important we take some time and appropriately understand this verse as it relates to prodigals.

I have read this verse in 35 different translations. One of the most commonly quoted is the King James Version, which is similar to most translations: "Train up a child in the way he should go; And when he is old, he will not depart from it."

Many parents of prodigals cling to this verse, and rightfully so. As a parent, you teach lessons, read scriptures, show a Christian lifestyle, and plant good seeds. Your heart has invested and loves this soul, only wanting good for your child. Your prodigal can reject or, as mentioned earlier, "suppress" the truth, but they know the truth. Remember, truth is not a set of information or faith. Truth is a person, and His name is Jesus.

"

YOUR CHILD IS CONTINUOUSLY BEING PURSUED BY GOD AND ENCOURAGED TO COME HOME.

I know of thousands of prodigals who have returned to God and been restored. Some did so relatively quickly, within years of walking away. But others spend decades as wayward sons and daughters of their Father in heaven. They were in their fifties and sixties, some even in their eighties, when they turned and walked home. I find this so encouraging! Why? Because the "hound of Heaven," as C.S. Lewis describes, never retreats. Your child is continuously being pursued by God and encouraged to come home.

As a parent, you give them a GPS with the coordinates for home already entered. They know home with God exists and, they can try to ignore it, dismiss it, and argue with it, but they know it is there. As a parent, however, you can't bend the scripture or the timeline. No matter how old your child is, it is the work of the Holy Spirit to reveal God to prodigals, and it could be decades before they return home.

A good friend of mine raised his children in a godly home. His son chose drugs, women, and was essentially homeless for over thirty years and one day came home. In a quiet and private moment with God, he stopped fighting the truth of God's love and total authority. He called his dad and said, "It's time I come home." The son has been restored as part of the family and participates in the family business.

> 66
> PAIN IS OFTEN THE FACTOR THAT
> BRINGS A PRODIGAL HOME.

I have worked with many sex-addicted prodigals who returned to God while in their fifties and sixties after they experience a tragedy. Remembers, as it was in the story of the prodigal told by Jesus in Luke 15, pain is often the factor that brings a prodigal home.

I'm not saying this to discourage you but rather to encourage you. I know every day that a prodigal is apart from God is one too many. However, if you're hopeless, distraught, frustrated (which is normal), see that God is at work, and you can be at peace. Proverbs 22:6 used the word "old" and not "older. And Proverbs affirms that wisdom and maturity come with time: "The glory of young men is their strength: And the beauty of old men is the grey head" (KJV). So, believe they will, by their old age (if not earlier), reflect on their life and choose to walk back to God.

My sister, like myself, was dropped off at the Salvation Army, but we were in no way raised in a Christian home. At fifty-four years old, her husband called me and asked me the weirdest question, "Doug, Suzie wants to know if you would do her funeral; she is at the hospital." My sister had a hard life and drank daily and smoked a lot. I went to the hospital, and that night she accepted Christ:

she died two weeks later. My sister had lived her entire life as a prodigal, but in her final days here on earth, she opened her heart to Christ. Her funeral included all the people she knew from the bars she frequented. It is important to remain in faith because even when they are old, they will know the way home.

> ## IT IS IMPORTANT TO REMAIN IN FAITH BECAUSE EVEN WHEN THEY ARE OLD, THEY WILL KNOW THE WAY HOME.

You can continue to pray and believe they will come home. You can trust the Father to do all He can do to have His son or daughter come home. Remember, He created them for his good pleasure.

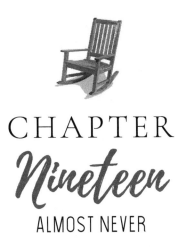

CHAPTER
Nineteen
ALMOST NEVER

Here I want to share an experience I have had with thousands of prodigals. Remember, I am a psychologist; my clients travel from all over the country and world and thus are from every type of background. I have heard thousands of stories of how a prodigal comes home. I have witnessed prodigals come home during a counseling session in my office. So, I want to share with you the process that is common to most and how this is very similar to the prodigal son story in the scripture.

This common thread begins with an external crisis which leads to an internal crisis. In a moment, expected or not, their world changes. It could be getting fired, being in a car accident, getting caught in affairs/pornography, or experiencing an economic disaster, family distress, a failing marriage, a personal health crisis, or a crisis with their own child. This external event creates an internal crisis. This internal crisis can be existential for the prodigal, leading them to ask,

"Who am I really?"
"What do I really believe?"
"What do I really want my life to look like?"
"What is the legacy I am leaving?"
"Who really is my God?"
"Who do I really love?"
"Why am I doing this?"

This internal crisis could also be more pragmatic for the prodigal.

"I can't get out of this without help."
"I can't figure it out."
"I can't pay this."
"I can't lie my way out of this."
"I have to face that I am limited, not God."
"I can't handle these consequences."

The external process creates an internal crisis that leads to the choices:

Hardening the heart

The most famous story of a heart repeatedly hardened was with the pharaoh (see Exodus, chapter 3 to 14). He would experience one judgement of God after another. Yet, he still held on to the idea that he himself was God until the last judgement. He, like a rattlesnake, would curl up instead of softening.

66

WHEN A PERSON BELIEVES IN LIES AT THE HEART LEVEL, AT THEIR CORE, THESE LIES BECOME PART OF THEIR IDENTITY...

A prodigal can take several big hits and still stay hard or even get harder. They choose to pull into themselves instead of reach out to their creator. A prodigal can suffer losses of several types because of poor choices and still be mad at God, you, or anyone who suggests they take responsibility for their life being a mess. Why? When a person believes in lies at the heart level, at their core, these lies become part of their identity and shape their view of themselves and the world they live in. Undoing this takes time, sometimes years or decades.

Shifting the heart towards God

When a heart shifts toward God, it starts to acknowledge its limitations. The heart starts to glorify God as God, which is where the prodigal went wrong in the first place. The heart cries out in some way—"I'm not God." "I'm tired." "I'm sorry"—and it reopens itself up to be led by a loving God. The heart acknowledges "heaven" like the prodigal son. They also acknowledge some of their sins. These confessions move the heart to pray, to cry to God, and to desire a community again. The softening of a heart toward God is a common sign that the heart has shifted. The heart is more open to hear and learn from God and others.

My experience is as the heart starts to move toward God, it starts to take responsibility for its choices and moves toward a more relational way of thinking and feeling (beginning to leave the object operating system behind).

Now, did you notice something that is not in the process of a prodigal coming home to God? Once again, do you see that as I briefly summarized the commonality of thousands of stories of real-life prodigals, there is something not present? Of course, you did! It is rare for parents to be directly involved in the coming home of the prodigal child. Now, I'm not saying after they come home to God, they don't come to seek you out because often they do. I'm identifying the specific moment or series of moments when reality hits or they are presented with the gospel and receive it. In those moments, rarely is a parent involved. Sometimes, it's a friend, a stranger who shares the gospel, a television preacher, their neighbor, a person at work, or even like the biblical prodigal, they stop suppressing the truth and just come to their "senses."

***

IT IS RARE FOR PARENTS TO BE DIRECTLY INVOLVED IN THE COMING HOME OF THE PRODIGAL CHILD.

You don't have to feel the pressure to be that person. You don't have to say the right thing or do the right thing for the prodigal to come home to God. You can pray for God to create or use circumstances as He wills. You can pray for God to send a messenger that your prodigal can hear. And be ready to celebrate when your child comes home!

"

YOU DON'T HAVE TO SAY THE RIGHT THING OR DO THE RIGHT THING FOR THE PRODIGAL TO COME HOME TO GOD.

I have seen so many parents of prodigals take on way too much responsibility for the prodigal to come home. Be thankful that God is using circumstances, consequences, and strangers to help your child. Your prodigal is on a journey, a journey only they can change. So, even if God doesn't use you directly, know He is moving on your child's behalf to bring them home to His own heart.

CHAPTER
Twenty
THE FATHER'S BEHAVIOR

The father in the prodigal son story is such an important person to watch in Jesus' parable. Earlier, we focused on the son in the parable. Now I want to spend a specific focus on the father. You see, he is a parent of a prodigal. I want to focus on the biblical example of the father in two of the prodigal accounts.

THE PARABLE OF THE PRODIGAL SON

Let's go to the prodigal story in Luke. The first thing we see is the father hears his son's request and accommodates it, giving his son the inheritance he demanded. Then the son left, which is what a prodigal with resources will often do. Now I want to look at what the father didn't do while his son went away and stayed away. Of course, as a father, he would have felt the grief and loss of his son. (I think he knew this particular son had to get his rebellion against God out of his system.)

The father never sent a servant to check in on him. The father never sent any money to bail him out. The father never helped on the journey back, and the father never coerced others to help his son.

"

HE ALLOWED HIS SON TO COME TO THE END OF THIS CRAZY PRODIGAL PROCESS ON HIS OWN.

So, what did the father do? He waited patiently. I'm sure, like you, he longed to see that boy walk up the driveway. He allowed the prodigal his own space. He did not spy on him, track him, or stalk him on social media. He allowed his son to squander money, make poor choices, and hit bottom all so he could, as the father hoped and perhaps believed, come to his senses. He allowed his son to come to the end of this crazy prodigal process on his own.

My point is, the father stayed on the porch. I'm sure he spent many nights looking off in the distance, feeling the pain and wondering if he should do something differently, but his choice was to do everything he needed to do to keep the home environment stable. I think he got up every morning and worked his farm. He kept the home a place his son would want to come back to. Sometimes, all parents of prodigals can do is the next right thing. Go to work, parent your other children, and keep life as normal as possible.

❝

THE FATHER STAYED ON THE PORCH.

Then the father in Luke 15:20, "But while he was still a long way off, he ran to his son, threw his arms around him and kissed him." This is one of my favorite parts of the story. Now, remember, the son walked for months. The father, like any parent, was ecstatic. His son, that was gone, is now home. The father heard the son's repentance but didn't acknowledge it at all. He responded, "But the father said to his servants, 'quick bring the best robe and put it on him. Put a ring on his finger and sandals on his feet. Bring the fatted calf and kill it. Let's have a feast and celebrate, for this son of mine was dead and is alive again! He was lost and is found' so they began to celebrate" (Luke 15:22).

There is no way to read these verses and not feel the joy of the father. He embraced his son, he clothed him, gave restored his honor as a son; these are all expressions of being relationally reconciled. The father celebrated the change of heart and the changes in his son's choices and welcomed him back.

66

THE FATHER CELEBRATED THE CHANGE OF HEART AND THE CHANGES IN HIS SON'S CHOICES AND WELCOMED HIM BACK.

This is the snapshot of what happens when prodigals come home broken, repentant, and humbled. You, too, will celebrate when your prodigal comes home.

THE FIRST PRODIGAL PARENT

I want briefly revisit the Father's behavior in the Garden of Eden, drawing your attention to how the Father responds when His children rejected His commandment and choose their own path.

What did the Father do after the fall? He gave His children clothes, had them escorted out of the garden, and allowed the natural consequences of their behaviors. He did not try to persuade them to stay. He did not attempt to undermine their future relationships so they would return. He let them go. He never left His children, but He allowed His children to leave Him.

Other than speaking directly to Cain, God did not have a recorded conversation with a man until Noah, which was several generations from Adam. Now, I'm not suggesting you don't talk to your prodigal or that you are not involved in their life. I am just showing you the Father allows the process to occur.

As parents of prodigals, each child, each situation, and each set of parent's motives are unique. What is helpful is how you, as parents, agree to go through the process with your prodigals.

> "
> BOTH FATHERS DID NOT TAKE RESPONSIBILITY IN ANY WAY FOR THEIR CHILDREN'S CHOICES.

I wanted to share these two examples of how the fathers responded. Both fathers did not take responsibility in any way for their children's choices. Each father let the prodigal process play out. Each father did not assist the prodigal while there were in their prodigal state.

I think there is wisdom as you look at the father's behaviors and apply that as you go through this chapter of your story with your prodigal.

CHAPTER
Twenty One
BOUNDARIES

The process of defining, establishing, and maintaining boundaries with prodigals can be a challenge. This can also be a place where a marriage, where there is not agreement, can get injured. Generally speaking, one parent will want to be soft, supportive, show their love by giving time, resources, and believing the best. The other parent will tend to be more principle-based and suggest limiting resources, allowing consequences, letting them pay their own bills, having more of a tough-love approach, and generally be more suspect of the prodigal's motives.

Now, you can clearly see how these two approaches will clash. It's important for parents to create agreed-upon boundaries they will adhere to when interacting with their prodigal. Breaking a boundary simply means that you and your spouse agreed to one thing, but one spouse decides to act outside of the agreement.

> **IT'S IMPORTANT FOR PARENTS TO CREATE AGREED-UPON BOUNDARIES THEY WILL ADHERE TO WHEN INTERACTING WITH THEIR PRODIGAL.**

Having outside accountability will help the marriage remain strong. An outside person can ask you legitimate questions as to why each of you believes what you do and is behaving in the way that you are. An outside person can challenge your compliance with the consequences for violating your boundary; you will respond to them differently than you would a spouse.

> **HAVING OUTSIDE ACCOUNTABILITY WILL HELP THE MARRIAGE REMAIN STRONG.**

Each situation is different, and your prodigal can be earlier or later in the process, have a serious addiction, mental issues, or none of these issues. However, you may need to have boundaries for the protection of the rest of the family and each other. The boundaries are also best for the prodigal. He or she knows where you stand as a team, and you are training them not to manipulate one person at the expense of the other. Also, you can punt to your accountability person, "We don't have an answer for you; we will check in with Pastor Jack and Sheri to see what they have to say about this issue."

Boundaries will be different for each situation and possibly each child if you have more than one prodigal. I want to provide a list of primary boundaries to give you a framework, to begin with as you create your own. You may also want to reflect on some of the biblical ideas presented in this book as you consider boundaries for your prodigal.

PRIMARY BOUNDARIES:
Money

Do we give any money to the prodigal? If so, for what? And why? Do they pay it back? Do we co-sign for loans for cars and housing? Do we give them cash or pay for items for them? Do we make purchases without the other spouse knowing?

Time

Do we need to limit interaction with the prodigal? If so, how do we manage this? Only public places? A certain length of time? Increments between visits?

Events

Do we invite the prodigal to family events, birthdays, weddings, or holidays? Do we discuss expectations if invited to events? Do we discuss bringing uninvited guests to events? Do we, in advance, discuss with the prodigal the consequences should their behavior be unacceptable?

Friends

Are their friends, sex partners, or addict friends permitted in our house?

There may not always be a clear right or wrong answer for each situation. What is important is that you agree and that you stick to the agreement. God, in explaining his expectations for His relationship with Israel, says, "Do two walk together unless they have agreed to do so?" (Amos 3:3). How can two walk together unless they are in agreement? This is probably the most important biblical principle to maintain as you, husband and wife, walk through the prodigal season.

> **❝**
>
> A SPOUSE THAT HAS SECRETS IN DEALING WITH THE PRODIGAL IS PREFERRING THEIR EMOTIONS AND THE PRODIGAL OVER THE SPOUSE.

A spouse that has secrets in dealing with the prodigal is preferring their emotions and the prodigal over the spouse—this will damage the marriage. You want to check your heart, motives, and beliefs if you are keeping secrets from your spouse. Elevating your prodigal and their issues above your spouse will be felt like a violation of "Love, honor, and cherish." If this is done repeatedly, you are intentionally hurting your spouse for the least mature person in your family. If you won't accept accountability for your behavior, I would seriously question why you are behaving in such a manner toward your spouse and your marriage. If you start keeping secrets from your spouse, this is dysfunctional and not honoring of your marriage.

It is not loving to keep someone from hitting the bottom and seeking God for help. It can prolong the process indefinitely. I know the anguish of letting them have pain or challenges in their life may seem difficult for you. However, long-term, having these short-term difficulties may be what they need to ask God for help.

Of course, having and keeping boundaries is very difficult because a prodigal can be anywhere on the spectrum of willingness to lie, manipulate, and use your love for them to meet or solve a problem in their life. Remember, confronting pain is the quickest way back to God. It is not the act of being rescued from the pain.

As a couple, and I have said this repeatedly, the parent prodigal journey may be one of the hardest things you go through as a couple. My encouragement is that you go through it together and make sure you are in agreement on the boundaries that are designed to protect your marriage and your family.

CHAPTER
Twenty Two
THE SIBLINGS

I want to draw your attention to the plight of the siblings of a prodigal. There is a person or several souls that often lay in the shadows of the prodigal story. They are scared, cry silently, and their pain is often overlooked during this prodigal saga.

When the prodigal rejects God and all those that in any way symbolize living under the reign of King Jesus, they often leave and reject their brothers and sisters. Depending on their past, gender, ages, and how bonded they were prior to the prodigal's choice to abandon them, their pain can be as deep as your own. The prodigal is your child and unique to you. As unique as they are to you is also how unique they are to each sibling.

The heart of each sibling has been torn and injured in the process of the prodigal's journey. Like the parents of the prodigal, the siblings endure very similar circumstances but with a much-added ingredient.

"

THE HEART OF EACH SIBLING HAS BEEN TORN AND INJURED IN THE PROCESS OF THE PRODIGAL'S JOURNEY.

They watch their prodigal sibling make bad choices in friends, sex, and drugs, much as you do. Sometimes they know way before you that the prodigal is walking away from God. They listen to the prodigal yell and act irrationally towards you and them. Remember that the siblings not only love the prodigal, they also deeply love you.

They hear the irrational and false blaming as the prodigal doesn't take responsibility for their poor choices in life and relationships. They are equally embarrassed and ashamed at the prodigal's behavior at family events or when the prodigal just doesn't care enough to show up.

They might also have shame and embarrassment because they have friends, neighbors, school people, and church people in common with their prodigal sibling. The siblings are often connected to the prodigal in so many relationships that the humiliation can be brutal and persist for years.

And it is common for siblings of prodigals to be judged by others as likely having the same bad attitudes and propensity to make the same poor decisions. This judgement is also a level of betrayal that many siblings experience and deeply resent. They feel falsely accused of a crime they had nothing to do with.

Additionally, these siblings are aware of your tears and the conversations and disagreements you have with your spouse (their mom or dad). They see the burden you carry as you go through the prodigal parent process. This is an added pain in each sibling's life that is a direct result of the prodigal's choice to reject God.

It is very difficult to watch your parents be ravaged by your sibling. So they not only carry their pain from the prodigal, they often daily feel your pain and how you don't deserve to be treated with such a lack of love and respect.

All of this can foster more anger and resentment towards the prodigal. And to be honest, they feel robbed because you can't be all you could be for yourself or for them. So, they conclude that because they are good, they should accept getting less of you, and this brings them more pain.

THE OLDER BROTHER

I want to spend some time examining the sibling part of the story of the prodigal son. I want to conduct this examination through the lens of the trauma this brother experienced. He lost his brother. He observed and likely felt his father's pain daily. He likely knew his younger brother's secrets and resented having to work harder on the farm as a consequence of the younger brother abandoning him and all the responsibility on the farm.

Every sermon I have heard on this parable that addresses the older brother presented the perspective that the older brother was judgmental and self-righteous towards his brother. I do not believe this was the point of Jesus' story.

The parent relationship with the child is unconditional by design. This is not the same as the sibling relationship. They did not birth their sibling. The sibling relationship is a choice relationship. They decide how to relate to a sibling.

> **THE PARENT RELATIONSHIP WITH THE CHILD IS UNCONDITIONAL BY DESIGN.**

As a person goes down the road of being a prodigal, they become the person you don't want your children to be around if they were not siblings. You would not demand that your child remain committed to a relationship with a peer of theirs that has rejected God, doesn't think clearly, makes bad choices, or is into drugs, sex, or other types of mischief.

If your other children are spiritually mature or sensitive, they sense that the prodigal is selfish and can't be trusted. When you force them to disobey what their spirit is telling them, it brings confusion to them. Let's go to Luke 15 again, starting in verses 25-36, "Meanwhile, the older son was in the field. When he came near the house, he heard music and dancing. So he called one of the servants and asked him what was going on. 'Your brother has come,' he replied, 'And your father has killed the fattened calf because he has him back safe and sound.' The older brother became angry and refused to go in. But he answered his father, 'Look! All these years I've been slaving for you and never disobeyed your orders. Yet you never gave me even a young goat so I could celebrate with my friends. But when this son of yours who has squandered your property with prostitutes comes home, you kill the fattened calf for him!'"

Many preachers preach this part of the story as if this good son was self-righteous or an equally bad sinner because he wasn't initially excited that his younger brother, who hurt everyone, came home. I contend that the older brother knew about his younger brother's habits and that he had a party and a woman problem. He knew where all the money was going to go. He knew his brother was irresponsible. He watched his father sit on the porch and pine for his rebellious and irresponsible all the while, he got up early and worked the farm daily.

Look at the beginning of the scripture, "Meanwhile, the older son was in the field." This responsible son was a hard worker, obedient to the father. Also, take a moment to evaluate his physical proximity. He was close enough to the father to hear the music at the house. This son was close to the father—not far off, rebellious, self-willed, and self-absorbed—unlike his younger brother. He didn't bring tears to his father. He didn't ask for something out of a spirit of entitlement. He was a good son. He had to do more work when his brother left. This is the hurt, anger, and resentment that most siblings of prodigals feel on a daily basis.

He didn't want to be around this self-absorbed brother. He wouldn't pick this type of person as a friend. As a parent, you wouldn't want this type of person around your children. The older brother needed more time to see change than a visit from the lost son, who had wasted everything.

"

THE SIBLING RESTORATION PROCESS CAN TAKE LONGER THAN THAT OF A CHILD BEING RESTORED TO THEIR PARENTS.

The sibling restoration process can take longer than that of a child being restored to their parents. You cannot rush this. Having seen and experienced the manipulation and wanting to be faithful to you, siblings are likely to be skeptical of their "one-prodigal's" motives and actions, thus they will take the time to observe the prodigal's relationship with you before beginning to trust their sibling again.

66

THE LAST THING THEY NEED IS TO BE INSTRUCTED TO FORGIVE THEIR PRODIGAL BROTHER OR SISTER.

They will probably have to do the anger and forgiveness work introduced earlier. The last thing they need is to be instructed to forgive their prodigal brother or sister. For the sibling, it's not so much about forgiveness as it is about trust. It is good to validate them, saying, "They betrayed you too, they lied about you as well, they ruined memories you can't ever get back. It's valid to feel hurt, betrayed and lied to. And it is okay to take time to heal."

The father shared his heart with the older brother in verse 31, "My son," the father said, "You are always with me, and everything I have is yours. But we had to celebrate and be glad, because this brother of yours was dead and is alive again, he was lost and is found." The father shared his excitement about his son returning. He also reassured the older brother that his inheritance didn't change because his brother was back.

What the father didn't do is shame him for not feeling excited. He didn't manipulate him with scriptures on the topic of forgiveness to make him feel guilty for not forgiving or that somehow now the older sibling is now the problem. The father didn't force a conversation between the two boys. The father trusted the process and the good heart of his older son. There is a lot of wisdom here on what the father didn't do.

"

THE FATHER TRUSTED THE PROCESS AND THE GOOD HEART OF HIS OLDER SON.

When we push the good child, without any validation of the pain they went through or the pain we went through, we are saying, "It doesn't matter how you feel. I don't care. I don't validate your pain. Your prodigal sibling is more important than you, yet again." This message is heard loud and clear by the other sibling, and the feeling of being less valued is reinforced one more time, solidifying the sibling's view that the prodigal has a higher place in your heart.

If you push too hard to have your "happy family" picture, you could push the good children away and make the process harder. So, be patient and not judgmental of your good children.

CHAPTER

Twenty Three

TAKING RESPONSIBILITY

In this chapter, I want to address a topic that some parents struggle with. What's my role? What did I do wrong? Now, talking from the prodigal's perspective, not the parents', there are many parents that haven't committed any serious wrongs. No, they aren't perfect, but they ask forgiveness when they should.

I've had so many prodigals say, "I had great parents," and as I addressed their family of origin, they were right. So, if you're that set of parents, still finish this chapter because you will probably be in a situation where this information can be helpful.

There are parents who have created pain regardless of intention to do harm. It is possible you have been:

- Physically abusive: overuse of physical discipline on your prodigal
- Physically neglecting: not meeting the physical needs of your prodigal
- Emotionally abusive: yelling at, name-calling, worthless statements towards your prodigal
- Emotionally neglecting: not allowing feelings to be expressed or identified by your prodigal
- Sexually abusive: excessive sexuality, sexual touch, or exposing of pornography Sexually neglecting: no sexual information given to your prodigal
- Spiritually abusive: no permission to ask spiritual questions, dogmatic without compassion toward your prodigal
- Spiritually neglecting: no spiritual direction given to prodigal

And, of course, there is a myriad of hurts and disappointments that may have caused pain, real or interpreted, by your prodigal while growing up in your home. And there is the reality that the prodigal, with their own thinking, can interpret any number of experiences any way they choose.

So, what do we do? May I suggest an exercise?

1. On a large piece of paper, draw a line down the middle, creating two columns

2. In the left column, write a list of the things you did or neglected to do that might have caused pain to your child

3. In the right column, write out how they might have felt during these experiences

4. Make an appointment with your prodigal to meet at a public place (this can keep it civil)

5. Review each incident separately.
   - What I did/didn't do?
   - How could you have felt?
   - Ask for forgiveness of each of these indicated

6. Enter the conversation with no expectations

Taking responsibility for any pain you caused is not like waving a magic wand that with resulting in your prodigal immediately changing and coming home. Taking responsibility will not guarantee anything will change in your relationship with your prodigal. It is simply the maturely taking of responsibility for your parenting decisions and actions. You taking responsibility is just you being an adult Christian owning any real sin you feel you committed. And where there are parents, each person should complete this exercise and conversation separately with the prodigal if it is felt necessary.

"

TAKING RESPONSIBILITY WILL NOT GUARANTEE ANYTHING WILL CHANGE IN YOUR RELATIONSHIP WITH YOUR PRODIGAL.

All you do is take responsibility. Your other children might have experienced similar things due to your immature behavior and not have chosen a path of a prodigal. You can't cause someone to be a prodigal.

This can also help you stop demeaning yourself up for not being a perfect parent. This exercise is freeing. I encourage you, complete this exercise when possible, but again, have no expectations of your child. You're just opening your imperfect heart to them. They will choose how they respond to this experience with you.

CHAPTER
Twenty Four
FORGIVING US

I love being human. I enjoy being able to live in an amazing body that can climb the mountains of Colorado, swim in the ocean, and otherwise play even as I approach sixty years young. I enjoy being able to worship our great God, hear music, think, rest, and even write to friends like you. I hope you enjoy being humans, free will and all.

However, being human does have a significant flaw. That flaw is we all sin. The scripture is clear that we all fall short. Thank God that Christ has come and delivered us from the penalty of sin.

The day-to-day reality is we all make mistakes. No, we might not have rejected God in the overarching sense of choosing to live as far from his as is humanly possible, but we have made mistakes relating to how we treat ourselves, our spouse, our children.

I am amazed how we Christians approach this whole topic of sin after we get saved. In some families or churches, they don't talk about sin in a practical way at all. Sin is the dirty little secret they know about but refuse to believe is happening in their circle. Of course, this approach is not helpful, be it personally, in the family, or church. And it is simply a denial of who God is and what He says about sin and humanity.

A second way some individuals, families, or churches deal with sin is to talk about other people's sins but never their own. In the first scenario, everyone agrees, most likely silently, that sin just doesn't exist. In this scenario, one person insists, often loudly, that sin exists, just not in their life. People who live like this have a very difficult time admitting they made a mistake or were wrong.

The biblical prescription for dealing with sin is to confess our sins to one another so we can be healed (James 5:16). When—not if—we sin, we must acknowledge, personalize and confess it so we can move on.

This makes quite a bit of sense when we sin against others, but what about when we hurt ourselves, sin against ourselves, or make significant mistakes in our lives. Then what do we do? I find that most people are more able and willing to forgive others than they are to forgive themselves.

I'd like to introduce you to another exercise. This is intended to clear all the plaque you have accumulated during adolescence, dating, marriage, or whatever journey you have walked through, including your current circumstances with your spouse, your prodigal, and any of your children.

"

WHEN WE FORGIVE OURSELVES, WE ACT, FEEL, AND BELIEVE IN GRACE...

When we forgive ourselves, we act, feel, and believe in grace experientially, not just philosophically or theological. It feels more real than just an idea. Too often, Christians sit in judgement of their own sins and fight an unnecessary battle inside themselves. The exercise will help you win that fight, and you will find the experience freeing. Now, you will remember that it is important that you do not judge the exercise until after you complete it.

Earlier I asked you to complete an exercise with two chairs facing each other to role play, forgiving your prodigal. If you did that exercise, this will be easy for you to do.

I want you to arrange two chairs, facing each other, again identified as chair one and chair two. Sitting in chair one, think and act and behave as yourself. Imagine another you in chair two. What I want you to do is ask forgiveness and take responsibility for the things you did or didn't do that you consider to be mistakes and sins. Include any secrets you have never told anyone, if you have any such secrets.

Address yourself by name. Ask for forgiveness. Be as specific as you can. Take your time. You might find this practice of asking for forgiveness to be mundane and thus be unemotional, or you might discover there is a wellspring of emotion that is ready to burst. Not knowing, I suggest having tissues nearby.

When you are done asking yourself for forgiveness for what you have done or haven't done, move to chair two. As you sit in chair two, you are also yourself. You heard you ask forgiveness for all the things you did or didn't do. Now, you get to respond. I want you to respond honestly to yourself. You might be challenged and say, "I am not ready. I'll get back to you." That would mean you're in the middle of the process, and you would repeat this exercise monthly until you are able to forgive yourself.

If you are able to extend grace and forgive yourself, then return to chair one and express gratitude for the forgiveness you have given yourself. Forgiving yourself is a significant and necessary measure of grace necessary to walk in freedom in your Christian journey. You don't want to unnecessarily carry or judge your own sins that were already forgiven. There is no freedom in self-condemnation.

"

FORGIVING YOURSELF IS A SIGNIFICANT AND NECESSARY MEASURE OF GRACE NECESSARY TO WALK IN FREEDOM IN YOUR CHRISTIAN JOURNEY.

You can also complete this role-play exercise with Jesus. I have had thousands of clients enjoy profound experiences with Jesus in the other chair. It's quite simple: Sitting in chair one, asking Jesus, in chair two, for forgiveness. Then, move to chair two and respond as Jesus has and promises to respond when the children of God as for forgiveness. Then return to chair one and express your thankfulness to Him. I strongly recommend you complete this exercise. You are likely to experience the incredible grace of Christ.

As a parent of a prodigal, the freer you are, the better for you and everyone around you. Your freedom will enable you to respond graciously to any guilt, false or real, you have.

"

YOUR FREEDOM WILL ENABLE YOU TO RESPOND GRACIOUSLY TO ANY GUILT, FALSE OR REAL, YOU HAVE.

As a child of God, you are entitled to freedom: "It is for freedom that Christ has set us free. Stand firm, then, and do not let yourselves be burdened again by a yoke of slavery." (Galatians 5:a). My hope is you do both of these exercises and receive this freedom into your life.

CHAPTER
Twenty Five
BLAMING

There is a devastating dynamic that can occur even in the best Christian marriages—blame. And it has been around since the beginning. Let's look at Genesis 3:8-13, which picks up after Adam and Eve chose to eat from the forbidden tree in the Garden of Eden.

> Then the man and his wife heard the sound of the Lord God as he was walking in the garden in the cool of the day, and they hid from the Lord God among the trees of the garden. But the Lord God called to the man, "Where are you?" He answered, "I heard you in the garden, and I was afraid

because I was naked; so I hid." And he said, "Who told you that you were naked? Have you eaten from the tree that I commanded you not to eat from?" The man said, "The woman you put here with me- she gave me some fruit from the tree, and I ate it." Then the Lord God said to the woman, "What is this you have done?" The woman said, "The serpent deceived me, and I ate."

Genesis 3:8-13

I love this story. Human nature instinctively blames. Adam blamed Eve. Eve blamed the serpent. Interestingly, God held each one accountable for their own choices.

Now for a moment, let's give this first sin event a context. They had the perfect relationship with the perfect father, perfect food, a beautiful garden to live in, and no notion of or examples of sin to follow. And when they disobeyed God, instead of taking responsibility, they went straight to the blame game.

As I gave the context of Adam and Eve, now let me give you some context for you as a parent of a prodigal. If married, you both are in trauma and feeling the pain of having a prodigal child. If you remember, depression, PTSD symptoms, anger, and all kinds of reactions of trauma are swimming in your souls. Both of you are enduring grief, can feel anger, will bargain, and be sad on a semi-regular basis. You are being challenged on how to process or explain how this became the outcome of your good parenting. You might have struggled with a false belief in cause and effect, or worse, believe that you failed to use your parental superpowers to control and protect your child. All of this is going on while you maintain all your responsibilities.

Then, the prodigal may do something, or the two of you will start talking about the prodigal, and the conversation gets out of control, and one or both of you could start attacking or blaming the other.

While this is a common attempt to manage grief, it is misguided and will hurt your marriage.

"

YOUR SPOUSE IS NOT RESPONSIBLE FOR YOUR PRODIGAL'S CHOICES, AND NEITHER ARE YOU.

So, what do you do? Hopefully, by now, you know your spouse is not responsible for your prodigal's choices, and neither are you: the prodigal process is between God and your child. However, you both may need to make amends for blaming each other now or in the past. There are cases where neither in the marriage blames the other or where one person blames, and the other doesn't, and yes, there are couples where both blame each other verbally or silently.

The same exercise you used to acknowledge, admit, and take responsibility for your behavior toward your prodigal, you can also complete while focusing on your relationship with your spouse. Take out a tablet of paper and start making your list of amends. On the left side of the paper, write down your blaming statements or beliefs. On the right side of the paper, write down how they would have felt when experiencing these. Be very specific about what you said to your spouse that blamed them for your prodigal's choices. You could also list some of the wrong beliefs you were keeping in your heart that you never expressed but wrongfully held onto.

Whatever your situation, if you feel it's appropriate, schedule a time in a public place to sit down and go through your list with your spouse. Then, make amends ask forgiveness from each blaming statement or idea that you believe you are guilty of.

TAKE THE TIME TO JOURNEY TOWARD FORGIVENESS, AND OFFER IT WHEN YOU ARE READY.

If, when you are on the receiving end of this exercise, your spouse is asking for forgiveness for something, you are honestly still in the process of forgiving, then when they ask your forgiveness, reply, saying you need more time. They don't need to come back to you. Their apology and request are sufficient. Take the time to journey toward forgiveness, and offer it when you are ready. If you can forgive what they are asking forgiveness for, then, of course, say, "I forgive you." It is a step in the right direction if you remove most of the plaque that has built up in your marriage because of blame. This can be helpful to unify you as a team through the storm of having a prodigal child.

CHAPTER
Twenty Six
THE MARRIAGE

Your marriage, other than your relationship with God, is the most sacred relationship you have. Remember that day standing before God and your family and friends promising to "forsake all others and to love, honor, and cherish each other?" That was a magical moment.

Your marriage has probably been through many challenges throughout the years. However, the challenge of a prodigal is often a prolonged and personal challenge. The potential impacts are depression, PTSD, addictions, quiet and fake guilt, only to name a few. Of course, these issues need to be addressed because they will inevitably impact the marriage.

Your marriage is weathering a long, unpredictable storm. Your love for them keeps you in this storm regardless of the specific circumstances. Now, I want to address with you the structure of a marriage. You have likely seen a movie with a ship in a storm. The structure of that ship will determine how well that ship will survive a storm. If the marriage structure is not maintained, the marriage can grow weak and be overcome while in the prodigal parent process storm.

> **IF THE MARRIAGE STRUCTURE IS NOT MAINTAINED, THE MARRIAGE CAN GROW WEAK AND BE OVERCOME WHILE IN THE PARENT PRODIGAL PROCESS STORM.**

As I cover each element of marriage, evaluate if this is a strength or an area to develop in your marriage.

Dating

Allow me to present a few helpful rules for dating I have been sharing in marriage conferences for decades.

You want to establish a frequency of dating weekly or biweekly. You probably don't want to date less than that. Also, you rotate responsibility for the date. When it is his date, he decides what he wants to do, and he is not trying to make his wife happy but make himself happy. When it's the wife's turn, she is making herself happy. You can create positive memories for your marriage, even through this storm.

> 66
> ## YOU CAN CREATE POSITIVE MEMORIES FOR YOUR MARRIAGE, EVEN THROUGH THIS STORM.

A date is not a place to discuss problems. A date is not shopping unless both people agree. A date is not running errands. A date is three or four hours of fun that that is more than a meal; it's fine to eat as part of a date, but it's more than eating.

Social

You don't need all your friends knowing everything that is going on; you may be able to trust some friends and not others with the sensitive details. Don't isolate yourself from your friends at this time. You both need time with same gender, Godly friends. You also need healthy married couples to walk through life with in every season of your marriage.

Spiritual

Of course, as Christians, you know to keep worshipping Him privately and publicly. Continue seeking God and feeding yourself the Word of God. Be a part of a local church so you can enjoy the corporate worship, sacraments, and opportunities to serve the church and the community.

Feelings

In every stage of life with your spouse, you want to be able to share your feelings with your spouse. If you are not good at this, I recommend my book *Emotional Fitness*. The more emotionally fit you both are, the better you will weather any storm that comes your way.

Sexuality

You want your sex life to be consistent, agreed upon, and growing over every season of your marriage. If one of the symptoms of this prodigal process or other marital issues is a problematic sex life, I recommend the book *Upgrade Your Sex Life*. In this book, I teach about sexual expression and help you discover your own and your spouses. You learn tips to have a great sex life and create a sexual agreement so you can have sexual peace instead of chaos. If the issues are severe, find a Christian counselor that addresses these issues specifically. If either of you is struggling with intimacy anorexia, google that term and get help for this issue.

Finances

Being in agreement financially on issues such as retirement, college, investing, savings, and how much debt to carry is very important. Having open communication about monthly finances is also important. Agree upon guidelines and regularly discuss finances as agreed upon. If this is an area of weakness, talk to your pastor about who in your church mentors couples on finances.

And new a few other general tips.

I am a firm believer in life-long learning and believe that reading marriage books at every stage of your marriage can help. This discipline keeps you focused on growing in your marriage. I have written several marriage books, which are available at www.drdougweiss.com.

Attend Christian marriage conference. By scheduling this time, it reminds you that your marriage is important and needs your loving attention. The teaching at these events is often biblically sound and personally applicable.

"

YOUR MARRIAGE IS IMPORTANT AND NEEDS
YOUR LOVING ATTENTION.

See a support group. Support during the storm of the prodigal parent process can be important for you and your marriage. If you don't have a prodigal parent process support group in your area, you can start one or at least have one couple you feel safe talking to.

CHAPTER
Twenty Seven
MY HOPE

When I started to talk about the prodigal parent process, I was amazed at how many Christian couples are in this process right now. When I started to research resources for parents of prodigals, I was amazed at how scarce they are.

My hope is you learned a lot about the prodigal process, and you accepted this is wholly between God and them. You did not cause this to happen; you cannot control this. You can pray for God to create the circumstances and send the right people to help. You can be in this for a long time. You don't have to be alone or ashamed. Your God loves your child. Your spouse and family have been impacted, and you can be a team as you walk together through the prodigal parent process.

If you have found this information helpful and healing as you walk this journey and you feel led to help other couples, reach out to your pastor and share your desire for there to be a ministry to parents of prodigals in your church. A bit of advice, I find pastors are much more willing to affirm and bless a ministry that already has compassionate leaders and a quality curriculum that they can approve of.

My prayer is that you both heal and grow strong in this season of challenge and experience Christ with you in this journey.

Appendix

MARRIAGE RESOURCES

LOVER SPOUSE

Lover Spouse helps you understand marriage from a Christ-centered perspective. Christian Marriages were designed to be different, passionate, fulfilling, and long-lasting.　　BOOK: $13.95

UPGRADE YOUR SEX LIFE

Upgrade Your Sex Life actually teaches you own unique sexual expression that you and your partner are pre-wired to enjoy.

BOOK: $16.95

SERVANT MARRIAGE

Servant Marriage book is a Revelation on God's Masterpiece of marriage. In these pages, you will walk with God as He creates the man, the woman and his masterpiece called marriage.

BOOK: $13.95

MARRIAGE MONDAYS

This is an eight week marriage training that actually gives you the skills to have a healthy and more vibrant marriage.

　　　　　DVD: $59.95

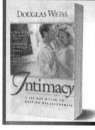

INTIMACY

This 100 Day guide can transform couples from any level of intimacy to a lifestyle of satiation with their spouse.　　　　BOOK: $11.99

MIRACLE OF MARRIAGE

God made your marriage to be an amazing and unique miracle. Dr. Weiss walks you through the creation and maintenance of your marriage. You will be exposed to a practical insights that can help make your marriage into God's original design.

BOOK: $12.95

OTHER RESOURCES

WORTHY: EXERCISES & STEP BOOK

The *Worthy* Workbook and DVD, is designed for a 12 week study. Here is a path that anyone can take to get and stay worthy. Follow this path, and you too will make the journey from worthless to worthy just as others have.

DVD: $29.95
BOOK: $29.95

EMOTIONAL FITNESS

Everyone has an unlimited number of emotions, but few have been trained to identify, choose, communicate, and master them. More than a guide for gaining emotional fitness and mastery, in these pages you will find a pathway to a much more fulfilling life.

BOOK: $16.95

LETTERS TO MY DAUGHTER

A gift for your daugher as she enters college. *Letters to my Daughter* includes my daily letters to my daughter during her first year of college.

BOOK: $14.95

BORN FOR WAR

Born for War teaches practical tools to defeat these sexual landmines and offers scriptural truths that empower young men to desire successfulness in the war thrust upon them.

DVD: $29.95

PRINCES TAKE LONGER THAN FROGS

This 2 hour DVD helps single women ages 15-30, to successfully navigate through the season of dating.

DVD: $29.95

SUCCESSFULLY SINGLE

This 2 Disc DVD Series is definitely nothing you have heard before. Dr. Weiss charts new territory as to the why for sexual purity.

DVD: $29.95

INTIMACY ANOREXIA

This hidden addiction is destroying so many marriages today. In your hands is the first antidote for someone with intimacy anorexia to turn the pages on this addiction process. Excerpts from intimacy anorexics and their spouses help this book become clinically helpful and personal in its impact to communicate hope and healing for the intimacy anorexic and the marriage.

BOOK: $22.95
DVD: $69.95

INTIMACY ANOREXIA: THE WORKBOOK

This is like therapy in a box. Inside is 100 exercises that have already been proven helpful in treating intimacy anorexia.

WORKBOOK: $39.95

INTIMACY ANOREXIA: THE STEPS

This is the only twelve step workbook just for intimacy anorexia. Each step gives you progress in your healing from intimacy anorexia.

STEP BOOK: $14.95

MARRIED & ALONE

This is for the spouse of an intimacy anorexic. You feel disconnected, untouched and often unloved. You are not crazy and Dr. Weiss will help you to start a journey of recovery from living with a spouse with intimacy anorexia.

BOOK: $14.95
DVD: $49.95

MARRIED & ALONE: HEALING EXERCISES FOR SPOUSES

This is the first workbook to offer practical suggestions and techniques to better navigate through recovery from your spouse's Intimacy Anorexia.

WORKBOOK: $39.95

MARRIED & ALONE: THE TWELVE STEP GUIDE

This Twelve Step guide will help the spouse of an intimacy anorexic work through the Twelve Steps that many others have found to be helpful in their recovery.

STEP BOOK: $14.95

SERIES FOR MEN

Every Christian man is born into a sexual war. The enemy attacks the young, hoping to scar them permanently and leave them ruined. Your past is not enough to keep you from the enduringly clean life you want and deserve. This series can be used individually or in a small group setting.

Every man can fight for and obtain a lust free lifestyle. Once you know how to stop lust, you will realize how weak lust really can be. God gace you the power to protect those you love from the ravages of lust for the rest of your life! It's time to take it back!

MEN MAKE MEN

Dr. Weiss takes the listeners by the hand and step-by-step walks through the creative process God used to make every man into a man of God. This practical teaching on DVD combined with the Men Make Guidebook can revitalize the men in any home or local church.

MEN'S RECOVERY

This book gives more current information than many professional counselors have today. In addition to informing sex addicts and their partners about sex addiction, it gives hope for recovery. The information provided in this book would cost hundreds of dollars in counseling hours to receive. Many have attested to successful recovery from this information alone.

BOOK: $22.95
CD: $35.00

101 FREEDOM EXERCISES

This is the best single resource for the Christian who desires to know what they need to do to get and stay free from sexual addiction. This book contains 101 exercises that have been proven to work. WORKBOOK: $39.95

STEPS TO FREEDOM

This is a Christian approach to the Twelve Steps. This book will guide you through the 12 Steps of recovery that have been helpful for many addicted people. This book is specifically written for the person desiring recovery from sexual addiction.
STEP BOOK: $14.95

HELPING HER HEAL

The *Helping Her Heal* DVD is for the man who has disclosed his sexual addiction to his partner or spouse. This DVD offers practical tools for hearing her pain, navigating her grief and losses, discovering her expectations of you and the boundaries she may need to heal.
DVD: $69.95

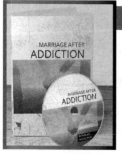

MARRIED AFTER ADDICTION

Addiction can have devastating effects on even good marriages. In this DVD you are intelligently guided through the journey you will experience if addiction is part of your marriage story. You will learn important information about the early and later stages of recovery for your marriage.
DVD: $29.95

WOMEN'S RECOVERY

Partners: Healing From His Addiction book is the latest in research of the affects on a woman who has lived with a sexual addict. The riveting statistics combined with personal stories of recovery make this a must read book for any woman in a relationship with a sex addict. This book gives you hope and a beginning plan for personal recovery.

BOOK: $14.95

PARTNER'S RECOVERY GUIDE

This is like therapy in a box for women who want to walk through the residual effects of being in a relationship with a sex addict.

WORKBOOK: $39.95

BEYOND LOVE

This is an interactive workbook that allows the partners of sex addicts to gain insight and strength through working the Twelve Steps.

STEP BOOK: $14.95

HE NEEDS TO CHANGE, DR. WEISS

He Needs To Change, Dr. Weiss DVD addresses the pain, trauma, and betrayal women experience because of their partner's sex addiction, betrayal, and/or intimacy anorexia.In this DVD, Dr. Weiss addresses the issue of change that he has explained to thousands of women in his office.

DVD: $29.95

UNSTUCK FOR PARTNERS

The *Unstuck* DVD is for every woman who has experienced the pain of their partner's sex addiction or intimacy anorexia and feels stuck, confused, frustrated and unable to move on. You didn't sign up for this and honestly, you don't get it! This DVD helps you "get it" so you can process the painful reality you are in and start to live again.

DVD: $29.95

PARTNER BETRAYAL TRAUMA

Partner Betrayal Trauma is real. Your pain and experience of betrayal has impacted all of your being and all of your relationships.

The book, DVD set, Workbook and Step guide were designed to help guide you thoughtfully through your own personal healing from the effects of being betrayed by your spouse or significant other. The pain and trauma of being betrayed, especially sexual betrayal, by a spouse or significant other is multidimensional and multifaceted. Your pain and trauma are real and these resources will help you in your journey of recovery from Partner Betrayal Trauma.

BOOK: $22.95   DVD: $65.95   WORKBOOK: $39.95   STEPBOOK: $14.95

RECOVERY RESOURCES

Recovery for Everyone helps addicts fight and recover from any addiction they are facing. Learn truths and gain a biblical understanding to break the strongholds in your life.

You will also find an explanation as to how an addiction may have become a part of your life and details as to how you can walk the path to recovery. You will find a roadmap to help you begin and navigate an incredible journey toward freedom. Then you can become part of the solution and even help others get free as well.

BOOK: $22.95   DVD: $99.00   WORKBOOK: $39.95   STEPBOOK: $14.95

RESOURCES FOR FEMALE SEX ADDICTS

Secret Solutions is a practical recovery exercise workbook written specifically for female sex addicts. Many of these techniques have been used in private practice to help other female sex addicts.

WORKBOOK: $39.95

She has a Secret book is the most current book in the field of sex addiction for women and is packed with new statistics to further our understanding of female sexual addiction. This is a must-read for any woman struggling in this addiction as well as for professionals in this field.

BOOK: $14.95

Heart to Heart Counseling Center has recently acquired Cereset, the most technologically advanced neuromodulation software available. It has received 13 peer review publications, and 9 Institutional Review Boards (IRB) clinically approved trials including the US Military.

By rebalancing and recalibrating the brain, it has helped anxiety, PTSD, trauma, sleeplessness, addiction, low mood and energy, TBI, stress management and neuroplasticity in many of my clients. Most spouses at Heart to Heart Counseling Center have many of the PTSD symptoms from betrayal. More than 80% of those with addiction have unresolved traumas as part of their story.

The brain is your central command center. When your brain is out of balance, or stuck, you don't feel right and it's impossible to function at your highest level. Cereset is a proven technology that's non-invasive and highly effective. Cereset can help your brain free itself, enabling you to achieve higher levels of well-being and balance throughout your life.

Here's what clients had to say about Cereset Garden of the Gods after their sessions:

> *"I'm waking up earlier and feeling more rested and alert. Anxiety is lessened. PTSD symptoms alleviated. Lessened food cravings and quantity of food reduced. Arthritis symptoms improved. I feel more relaxed, less angry and reactive."*

The cost for five sessions (one per day) is $1,500.

For more information call us at 719-278-3708

A·A·S·A·T

American Association for Sex Addiction Therapy

SEX ADDICTION TRAINING SET

Both men and women are seeking to counsel more than ever for sexually addictive behaviors. You can be prepared! Forty-seven hours of topics related to sexual addiction treatment are covered in this training including:
- The Six Types of Sex Addicts
- Neurological Understanding
- Sex and Recovery
- Relapse Strategies

TRAINING SET: $1195

PARTNER'S RECOVERY TRAINING SET

With this AASAT training, you will gain proven clinical insight into treating the issues facing partners. You can be prepared! Thirty-nine hours of topics related to partners treatment are covered in this training, including:
- Partner Model
- Partner Grief
- Anger
- Boundaries

TRAINING SET: $995

INTIMACY ANOREXIA TRAINING SET

This growing issue of Intimacy Anorexia will need your competent help in your community. Now, you can be prepared to identify it and treat it. In this training you'll cover topics like:
- Identifying Intimacy Anorexia
- Causes of Intimacy Anorexia
- Treatment Plan
- Relapse Strategies

TRAINING SET: $995

FOR MORE INFORMATION VISIST WWW.AASAT.ORG OR CALL 719.330.2425

NEW PRODUCTS

NARCISSISM SEX ADDICTION AND INTIMACY ANOREXIA

The profound information that you will learn in this DVD will help you fairly evaluate your specific situation for narcissism, which will help you develop a treatment plan to address the issue you are dealing with at its core. Having this clarity can help expedite the healing process for the sex addict, intimacy anorexic, and the spouse, as they are able to tackle the real issue at hand.

DVD: $29.95

DISCLOSURE

Disclosure is one of the most important topics in sexual addiction recovery. In this DVD, Dr. Weiss discusses the various types of disclosure. Each type of disclosure is for a specific purpose or person. This DVD can expedite the understanding of each of the significant processes of disclosure for the addict, the spouse and the marriage.

DVD: $39.95

BOUNDARIES

Boundaries are a healthy, normal, and necessary part of the recovery process for sex addicts, intimacy anorexics, and their spouses. In this DVD set, Dr. Doug Weiss provides an answer to the clarion call on boundaries by educating and guiding you through this process.

DVD: $49.95

SIN OF WITHHOLDING

This DVD is the first to address the Biblical foundation of the sin of withholding in believers' hearts. The practical application in marriage addressing Intimacy Anorexia is also interwoven in this revelational teaching on the Sin of Withholding. Once a believer is free of this sin, their walk with the Lord and their fruit towards others can increase expediently.

DVD SET: $49.95

PAIN FOR LOVE

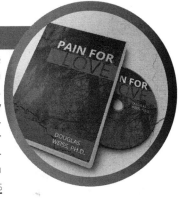

Pain For Love describes in detail one of the most insidious strategies of an intimacy anorexic with their spouse. This dynamic is experienced by many who are married to an intimacy anorexic. This paradigm can empower the spouse and help them stop participating in a pain for love dynamic in their marriage.

DVD: $29.95

HEALING HER HEART AFTER RELAPSE

Relapse doesn't have to occur, but if it happens, knowing how to navigate it intelligently can make a huge difference in a marriage. Each relapse impacts the wife significantly.

This DVD is way more than, "He relapses, he does a consequence and moves on." The addict is given real tools to address the emotional damage and repair of her heart as a result of a relapse. Every couple in recovery would do well to have these tools before a potential relapse.

DVD: $29.95